A Sabbath Shared

Father Chet Snyder

authorHOUSE®

AuthorHouse™
1663 Liberty Drive, Suite 200
Bloomington, IN 47403
www.authorhouse.com
Phone: 1-800-839-8640

First published by AuthorHouse 11/25/2008

ISBN: 978-1-4389-3336-8 (sc)
ISBN: 978-1-4389-3337-5 (hc)

Printed in the United States of America
Bloomington, Indiana

This book is printed on acid-free paper.

Scripture Quotations from the New American Bible. United States Conference of Catholic Bishops, 3211 4th Street, N.E., Washington, D.C. 20017-1194

DEDICATION

Dedicated to the memory of my parents, Chester Graham and Kathryn Marian, whose open hearts and loving home provided a Sabbath rest for all who shared their lives, and to Mike and Rose and Sue and Tom, who continue the tradition of our parents in opening their homes to me as a place of Sabbath rest.

From sunset to sunset, the Sabbath withdraws man from the world of work and transfers him to the world of pleasure; from the world of tension to the world of delight; from the world of doing and making to the world of being. (Rabbi Theodore Friedman)

CONTENTS

Jerusalem

Istanbul

Sailing the Aegean

Athens

London

AUTHOR'S PREFACE

Place has always been important to me: my parent's kitchen table, the seminary chapel, a lounge chair at a favorite beach. Some people are happy wherever they are. I, on the other hand, am more particular about where I find myself. I breathe more easily, think more clearly and pray more fervently when the environment is to my liking. That is why, when I decided to take a sabbatical, I took great care in deciding where I would be for my five month "Sabbath."

As a student in Rome, I fell in love with the art, history and culture of the Italian people. I like to say that I am Italian by choice, if not by birth. When I arrived as a pilgrim on my first trip to Jerusalem in 1975, I felt as if I had come home. It was not surprising, therefore, that I chose to spend a significant amount of my sabbatical time in the Eternal City and the Holy City to walk in the footsteps of Jesus and the footsteps of Peter. If my mother had her way, I would have been called "Paul." To please her, I later selected "Paul" as a Confirmation name. Now, many years later, I decided also to walk in the footsteps of my patron at the conclusion of my Sabbath journey.

This book is a way for me to share the fruit of my sabbatical with others in the hope that the blessings I received during this privileged time will be a grace for my readers as well.

The sabbatical was made possible by the generosity of Bishop Kevin Rhoades of Harrisburg, Pennsylvania who granted me the time away for rest, reading, prayer and travel. I am also grateful to the Lilly Endowment for awarding me the Clergy Renewal Grant which funded my sabbatical journey.

I would like to thank my friend and mentor, Father T. Ronald Haney, for encouraging me to write and publish my reflections. I am also grateful to my friend Mary Shriver for helping me with the manuscript, and to family and friends whose kind words and loving prayers supported me during my time of extended Sabbath rest.

A Journey Begins

After years of dreaming and months of planning I will be leaving on a jet plane in just a few more hours to begin a five month sabbatical. This past week I called a credit card company to report that I would be traveling out of the country. When I listed the dates and locations, the attendant gasped, and before collecting her composure and returning to her professional mode she said: "Wow, all those places, all that time. Why are you going?" Why indeed?

The answer is easy – rest, study, prayer, writing, travel to new places. Yes, but *why*? Because the human spirit in all of us needs to "Sabbath" –to break from the routine, however significant that routine might be; to catch one's breath, however breath-taking life is; to see things from a new vantage point, however advantageous our life situation might be.

Sometimes we "Sabbath" for a few minutes at the end of a busy day when we think about the blessings and challenges the day has brought to our doorstep. Sometimes we "Sabbath" for a day when we take the Lord at his word and make holy his day with worship and rest. Sometimes we "Sabbath" for a week when we gather with family and friends and play at the beach, hike in the hills or travel to lands on our list of places to see before we die. And sometimes we are blessed enough to carve out an extended time, not to run away from, but rather to turn around and see from afar what our world has been.

It is what Jesus did when he wandered on the hillside at the end of a day's preaching to enter into communion with his Father in heaven. It is what Mary did when she went to the hill country of Judea to be with Elizabeth her kinswoman who, like her, was cooperating with the mysterious plan of God. It is what a married couple does when they go out on a date or journey away for a second honeymoon. It is what we all do when we stop taking ourselves too seriously and allow quiet and play and prayer to be the serious business of the day.

It is my hope, in the days and weeks and months ahead, to share some of my Sabbath sabbatical with you. While there is something of an agenda – prayer, study, writing, rest – I believe that the most significant blessings of this time will be the surprises that the Lord has in store me.

A long time ago in a place far away the Lord God Yahweh told Moses on the mountain: "Take off your sandals. The place where you are standing is holy ground". About an hour ago an airport security guard barked: "Take off your shoes and put them in the baggage tray". I must admit, the Newark airport does not look like holy ground! But I know that in each place I visit in Rome, Jerusalem, Greece, and Turkey, following in the footsteps of Jesus, Peter, Paul and countless other pilgrims who have gone before me, I, too, like Moses will be invited in surprising ways to see the face of God.

Welcome to all who will travel with me. Now, let us begin…

Rome

The Street Where I Live

Like most major metropolitan areas, Rome is a city of neighborhoods, each with its own personality depending on its history, its positioning and above all else, the make up of its people.

I am staying in the section of Rome called the "Borgo". Most people visiting Rome pass through the Borgo of their way to the Vatican without giving it much notice. But the Borgo is more than a thoroughfare to Saint Peter's. It is a place where people live, work, meet friends, raise children, go to dinner and talk about football – what we in the United States call soccer. Perhaps that is the appeal of the Borgo for me and why I chose to stay there during my sabbatical. Certainly being close to Saint Peter's Basilica and the Vatican Museum is an added bonus. But experiencing life happening all around me each day is also a great blessing.

The Borgo had its beginning in the early Middle Ages when the Saxons established it for themselves upon arriving in Rome. The name "borgo" derives its meaning from the same Saxon word from which we get "borough". I am staying at the Hotel Santa Anna on the Borgo Pio. In addition to being charming, the hotel has a sentimental value for me. It is where my mother and a dear friend stayed in July of 1974 when they visited me while I was a student and where I have stayed with friends on return visits to the city.

Each morning the street comes alive with people rushing to work, children leaving their apartment for school (everyone in Rome lives in an apartment) and priests and sisters in all styles of ecclesiastical garb making their way to the Vatican to so who knows what! This morning, my first full day here, a group of men gathered in the middle of the street to eat pizza bianca and solve the problems of this wonderful, historical city, filled with life with all its surprises and contradictions.

Because Wednesday is the day of the Papal audience there is more traffic than usual. But the residents of the Borgo take it all in their stride. After all, they knew Benedict XVI was he was their good neighbor Cardinal Ratzinger, shopping in their stores and sharing day to day life in their neighborhood, one among many in a city that attracts millions of visitors each year, but home to only a select few. How bold of me to think of myself as one of them, even if it is for only seven weeks!

Still Christmas In Rome

The world credits Saint Francis of Assisi with making the first Nativity scene. And the Italians of today would make this beloved Saint proud of the way they have carried on his tradition. During the Christmas season every church in Rome displays a "presepio", each more grand than the next.

Some churches, like Saints Cosmas and Damian in the Roman Forum, keep the display up all year long. Theirs is a Neapolitan presepio made up of hundreds of hand crafted figures taking up an entire room. Admission charge: two euro!

Pope John Paul II revived a tradition of having a nativity scene in Saint Peter's Square, where it remains until the Feast of the Presentation of the Lord on February 2, forty days after Christmas. The figures are life-size and show the Holy Family under a Bedouin tent raised on the side of a cave. They are surrounded by angels, shepherds, the magi and people from the village all going about their daily work. The scene is most effective at night when those entering the square are greeted by a large, lighted Christmas tree and the presepio bathed in light. The humble village scene is made all the more dramatic as seen against the backdrop of the majestic baroque exterior of Saint Peter's Basilica.

Also, there is an interesting contrast created by the large Christmas tree positioned next to the Egyptian obelisk in the center of the square. The obelisk was brought to Rome from Alexandria by the emperor Caligula in 37 A.D. A few years later Nero had it placed in the center of his circus, located next to the Vatican Hill. In 1586 Pope Sixtus V moved it to its current location. Saint Peter was martyred in the circus of Nero circa 67 A.D. That means that the obelisk may well have been the last thing Saint Peter saw before his martyrdom.

One cannot walk in Rome without meeting myth, folklore, history, tradition and faith around every corner. Ancient and modern, pagan and Christian all come together and present pilgrims with sensory overload with each step they take along the cobblestones. It is why Rome is eternal and is, in large measure, why I am drawn here.

My First Sunday In Rome

One of my favorite childhood memories is the feeling associated with life slowing down on the weekend. Early on Saturday mornings my mother, who worked during the week, would do laundry, catch up on housework and either she or my father would grocery shop for the week. But by mid-day life began to slow down and most work activity stopped. And certainly by Sunday life was lived at a different pace. Our main meal together as a family was at noon and the rest of the day was spent reading the Sunday papers, watching television or going for a ride in the countryside to "spot deer" with my father, the hunter. All stores (including grocery stores) were closed so there was no thought of shopping. Sunday was morning Mass, a family meal and rest. Perhaps that is why the theme of Sabbath rest is so important to me as an adult as I see the pace of life on Sunday for many people being no different from the rest of their work week.

That having been said, how strange this first weekend of sabbatical when there is nothing I am required to do. Weekend life in parish ministry is, of course, filled with activity. Masses, confessions, baptisms and weddings are all part of the blessings of priesthood that we share with parishioners in great numbers. And so on Saturday I asked myself: "How do you want to spend tomorrow? After all, this is *your* chance to 'have a restful Sunday!'" So, let me tell you what it was like.

I went to Mass at Saint Anne's, the parish church of Vatican City, just a block from my hotel. There were only about 60 people in this beautiful little church which could have held three times that number. Except for one family with two small children, the "rest of us" were over 50, some more than others! Mass was celebrated by some Bishop who did not identify himself (bishops are everywhere in Rome!) and the homily was given by a priest who looked like everyone's Italian grandfather! Taking his lead from the gospel story of the wedding feast of Cana, his homily was about Mary as Mother of the Church, leading and helping all of us to follow her Son. "Do whatever he tells you," we were reminded as we make our way through the challenges of life together.

After a lovely breakfast of café latte and a cornetto (pastry) at the local (coffee) bar, I "rested" for two hours with a wonderful book about the Psalms. I then made my way to St. Peter's Square for the noon blessing of the Holy Father, a weekly event.

It seems that anyone who is anyone comes to the Square for the praying of the Angelus and the Pope's Sunday blessing. People of all ages from all corners of the world gather to hear a brief message in Italian from the Holy Father, who also offered a summary in French, English, German, Polish and Spanish. We prayed the Angelus and Pope Benedict offered us his blessing and then made his way from the window for, I suspect, a lunch of spaghetti or sauerkraut!

I had spaghetti at a favorite restaurant and then walked around the city taking pictures for a few hours. Italians love to walk (*fare una passagiata*) on Sundays and there were many families enjoying the mild weather. I would note that most, although not all, stores were closed!

I ended that walk near a favorite spot, the Ponte San Angelo or Angel Bridge leading across the Tiber to the Castle San Angelo. At his noon blessing Pope Benedict made note of this being Migrant or Immigrant Sunday. He spoke of the importance of seeing immigration not simply as a *problem*, but rather as *people* who are longing for a better way of life. He also spoke about our responsibility as Christians to promote the dignity of all people, especially families who are seeking a way of life together that is free from poverty and oppression. His words came to life at the Bridge and Castle as many (I am sure, undocumented) Africans were selling "Gucci" purses and "Burberry" scarves. A tour guide told us recently that many Africans enter the country and begin life selling goods on the streets of Rome until they have enough money to move to the northern industrial cities where they are needed in the factories. One of the reasons they are needed is because the Italian birth rate is so low and the population is aging.

I thought about our own country and found the words of the Holy Father to be challenging as we wrestle with questions of immigration and national security. And I could not help but wonder if we might also be concerned with our own financial security – will there be enough to go around if more people are allowed to change their status to "documented." I do think that the voice of our church is needed at this critical time so that we do not allow our fears to overshadow the gospel call to justice spoken so clearly by Jesus when he said "I was a stranger and you took me in."

Buona Domenica a tutti!

Keep Your Eyes And Ears Open

One of the many blessings of my sabbatical thus far has been having leisure time to walk around the city of Rome in unhurried fashion. Understandably, on other visits here I felt pressured to run from one site to another in order to see as much as possible. But these past days I have wandered around the busy streets of a nation's capital and the narrow passageways of a sometimes sleepy city and enjoyed sights and sounds always there, but easily missed. Let me share some of these hidden treasures with you.

I took a picture of a nearby bridge while crossing the "Ponte Garibaldi" from Trastevere to the city's center. Everyday tens of thousands of people cross this very busy bridge in cars, busses and on foot. I wonder how many notice the next bridge over. The "Ponte Fabricio" connects Tiber Island with the "mainland" and asks the question "How old is old?" Still used by pedestrians it is also known as the "Ponte dei Quattro Capi" and was built in *62 B.C.*, making it oldest bridge in Rome. It makes this pastor wonder why, in our society, it is often less expensive to "tear down the old and build the new" while in this eternal city what was constructed more than two millennia ago still works!

It is hard to really get lost while walking in Rome. Even the narrow back streets and alleys, removed from the beaten path, eventually lead back to a major "via" or "corso." Last Sunday, while walking back to the hotel after a leisurely meal and stroll through the city, I was enjoying the peace and quiet of the deserted back streets. But as I turned a corner I heard the sound of a distant accordion. I "followed my ears" and soon found a lone street musician playing his heart out. It didn't seem to matter that no one was near. He played with heart and abandon and seemed pleased when he realized someone was listening and enjoying his music. I tossed a few coins into his hat and asked if I could take his picture. He smiled and said "si, certo" and went on playing as if he had found a new friend.

Except for the early morning and evening hours, Saint Peter's Square is bustling with tourists or "cittidini" who pass through on their way to work on the other side of the piazza. Entrance to Saint Peter's is through metal detectors (a sign of the times in which we live) placed on the right side of Bernini's splendid colonnade encircling the square (is that an oxymoron?). There is another spot that thousands of people pass by and never see because they hurry on their way and never look down. For just to their left, as they enter the barricade leading to the metal detectors, is a small marble plaque set amid the cobblestones. It has the date May 13, 1981 and the coat of arms of Pope John Paul II. It marks the place on the piazza where the Holy Father was shot on that ominous spring day, a reminder to the world of the unsettling, often violent times in which we live. It is also a reminder of the spirit of this giant of faith who later met with his attempted assassin in his prison cell and offered him forgiveness.

This leisure time challenges me to ask how many times I miss the treasures all around me because the pace of life is so hurried. It might be my neighbor's well-kept garden, the laughter of our school children at recess play or the constellation Orion that hovers over my driveway on a cold, crisp winter night. Maybe upon my return I will be more careful to see what little miracles are all around me and not just hurry off to the next task to be done.

One more treasure to share with you. Amid the street signs on the corner of a building where the Borgo Pio meets the Vicolo del Campanile just three blocks from my hotel, there is a shrine with an 18th century painting of the Madonna and Child. Just below the shrine is a plaque announcing that Pope Pius VI (Angelo Braschi) in 1797 promised 200 days plenary indulgence to anyone of either sex ("del uno e l'altro sesso") who prayed the litany of the Blessed Virgin under the shrine. I have not yet found such a promise to "only" men or to "only women"! But in this city, who knows, anything is possible. I will keep "looking up" and "looking down" and if I find one I will let you know!

Blessing Of The Lambs

Saint Agnes, Virgin and Martyr, was murdered in the year 304 A.D. in Rome in the Stadium of Domitian, now the famed Piazza Navona. She was buried in a catacomb along the Via Nomentana. In the fourth century, Constantina, a daughter of Constantine, had a church built over the sight in gratitude for a healing she received while praying at the grave of Agnes. That church was restored by Pope Symmachus in the 5th century and completely rebuilt by Pope Honorius in the 7th century. Later restorations were done in the 19th century by Pope Pius IX. But the church as it stands today is essentially the church of the 7th century and is a perfect example, along with other significant churches like St. Clement, and St. Prassede, of what a "basilica" of that period looked like in Rome at that time.

The Basilica of Saint Agnes Outside the Walls (San Agnese fuori le Mura) is also an active parish church. It is interesting to visit the 7th century church, the catacomb underneath and the 4th century church of Santa Costanza on the same grounds, and then see the modern parish bar and bocce court next door!

Because the Basilica is off the beaten path (two kilometers beyond the ancient city walls) visitors usually do not see many other people there. However that was not the case on January 21, the feast day of Saint Agnes, when thousands came to the 10:30 Mass for the Blessing of the Lambs. There were people everywhere, crowding the aisles and sitting at the base of the 7th century marble columns. The younger children were invited to sit around the altar as Cardinal Camillo Riuni, the Pope's Vicar for the diocese of Rome, celebrated the Mass and Blessing in this, his titular church.

The first written record of the Blessing of the Lambs dates to 1442. It is a ceremony that combines tradition and a popular piety that makes our Catholic Church so rich in its spiritual history.

The lambs are brought to the Basilica from the Trappist Monastery at Tre Fontane, built over place where Saint Paul was martyred about 67 A.D. The two lambs are placed on a pillow in a wicker basket richly decorated with garlands and flowers. One lamb wears a crown of white roses, the other a crown of red roses, symbolic of Saint Agnes as Virgin and Martyr. They were carried in procession by young girls and placed on the altar where they were blessed by Cardinal Riuni. The lambs are shorn on Holy Thursday and the wool is taken to the Benedictine Sisters at Saint Cecilia in the Trastevere section of the city. The wool is then woven into the "pallia", a special vestment worn by archbishops in the church. Traditionally new archbishops receive the pallium from the pope at ceremony of investiture on June 29, the Feast of Peter and Paul. The day before, the pallia to be distributed are placed in an urn next to the tomb of Saint. Peter. The pallium is a kind of collar that is worn over the chasuble when the archbishop celebrates Mass within his own diocese. The Holy Father, as universal pastor, wears the pallium wherever he celebrates Mass. Pope Benedict XVI wears a pallium that is considerably more substantial than other popes have worn in recent times in a style that goes back centuries.

It was thrilling to experience this ceremony so rich in history and tradition. As Catholic people we are dependant on signs and symbols to help us understand the deeper meaning of our faith. In this case, archbishops have a special role to play in pasturing the sheep of Jesus' church in a manner that reflects the virtue and courage of Saint Agnes, herself a "lamb" who was sacrificed for her virtue and faith. At the ceremony I offered special prayers for Sister Agnes Marie, who by her teaching and example helps the young children of Saint Joseph School in Mechanicsburg grow in appreciation of the love that Jesus has for each one of them, a sheep of his fold.

Some Thoughts On Prayer

I give thanks to my God at every remembrance of you, praying always with joy in my every prayer for all of you, because of your partnership for the gospel from the very first day until now. (Philippians 1:3-53)

Before leaving Mechanicsburg I promised family, friends and the congregation at Saint Joseph Parish that I would remember them in prayer during my sabbatical. Let me share with you some of the ways that I have been keeping that promise.

I have been thinking a lot about prayer these first two weeks away. Prayer is, above all else, remembering that God is with me. And so I have been taking time to remember what is true even when I am unaware of it: God *is* with me. When I pray I allow myself not only to *remember*, but to *be* in God's presence. It is like spending time with a friend. There is activity and conversation, shared memories and hopes and concerns. But at some point the activity stops, the conversation ends and a quiet enters in. And when that happens I simply enjoy *being with* my friend.

And it is the same with prayer. Sometimes the Lord's presence is known in the hundreds of thoughts and images that enter my mind while praying. Far from being distractions, those images remind me of the richness of my life and the challenges I face in daily living. When that happens I am invited to let the Lord in on the particulars of what has been today and will be tomorrow, remembering that I do not walk alone.

Sometimes God's presence is known in the peace and quiet that prayer can bring; allowing me to set aside the busyness of life for a time and rest in the Lord's gentle embrace. I usually treasure those moments, so different from the pace of a hectic day or thoughts of a thousand things to do tomorrow. When the quiet happens, I simply enjoy being in the presence of my friend, who is also my God.

When I pray for others, whether my mind is racing or my heart is quiet, I am inviting them into my awareness of God's presence. It is like introducing one friend to another. Is there any greater joy than bringing together people we love? In prayer I bring together the people I love and the God I love, and allow them to enjoy one another's company while I watch with delight.

Let me share with you some of the places where I have been praying for all who are close to me.

First, up the street and around the corner to Piazza San Pietro surrounded by Bernini's colonnade. On top of the colonnade there are statues of 88 saints. I do not know who any of them are! Except one. On the left hand side, eighth from the end, stands Saint Joseph, joining the others who watch over the thousands of visitors who make their way through the Square each day. Each time I cross the Square I look up to Joseph and pray for the people of Saint Joseph in Mechanicsburg who share life and faith with me each day. And I pray for the faithful people of my home parish of Saint Joseph in Shamokin (now Our Lady of Hope) whose example first introduced me to life in Christ.

Saint Peter's Square is not the only place to find Joseph in Rome. In the heart of the city the Jesuit Church (Il Gesu) is a masterpiece of the Baroque style, splendid and triumphant in every inch of its massive interior. However there is one side chapel that is easy to miss. It is home to Pietro Gagliardi's painting of the Holy Family of Nazareth in the Workshop of Saint Joseph. There I pray for all families, my own and those in the parish I pastor. And I pray in a special way for those families that know tension and turmoil, disappointment and uncertainty, division and loss.

In that same church, in a chapel that cannot hide, is the tomb of Saint Ignatius of Loyola, founder of the Society of Jesus, the Jesuits. The splendor of the chapel and tomb is a fitting tribute to the giant of faith that Ignatius was in his day and still is today through the influence of his followers and the gift they are to the Church. I was taught by the Jesuits at the University of Scranton and in Rome and so at the tomb of Ignatius I pray for his followers who taught and influenced me. I also pray for all teachers in whose hands we place our most precious gift, the children that God has given to us.

Not too far from "Il Gesu", a stone's throw from the Pantheon and the Piazza Navona, is another favorite place, the Church of Saint Augustine. Not many visitors to Rome get to see this church since it is overshadowed by the four major basilicas and some of the other larger churches in the city. But San Agostino, built in the 16th century, is rich in history and the treasures it contains. At the entrance is a statue called the Madonna del Parto, or Madonna of Childbirth. Here pregnant women, those experiencing a difficult pregnancy, and those hoping to be with child come to pray, seeking Mary's intercession so that they too, like her, will be blessed with a child. Surrounding the statue are silver hearts, traditionally placed there by those who prayers have been answered. I try to visit San Agostino whenever I come to Rome to pray at this statue for those women and couples I know who long to share the gift of their life and love with children. So for all of you who share that longing, know that I have prayed for you, introducing your names and intentions to Mary, the Mother of Jesus. Meanwhile I stand back and watch with delight as she watches over you.

At the front of the San Agostino in a chapel in the left transept under the altar, is the tomb of Saint Monica, the mother of Saint Augustine. Monica died in 387 A.D. in Ostia, the seaport of the city of Rome. We all know her as the woman whose constant prayer for her Son finally lead to his conversion and his becoming one of the most important theologians and bishops in the early days of Christianity. Monica stands as an example of what the New Testament means when it says that we are to pray constantly, with hope, not losing heart. I pray at the tomb of Monica for all of our family members and friends whose lives are without direction, those who struggle with faith, and for those who have known confusion and hurt and have left the church. Like Monica, we pray with hope and entrust our loved ones to God's guidance and care, remembering the words of the Fourth Eucharistic Prayer: "We pray for those whose faith is known to you alone."

There is one other place in San Agostino that is special to me. In the nave, on the third pillar on the left, there is a fresco of the prophet Isaiah painted by Raphael in 1512. It has recently been cleaned and it is splendid. It is said that the man who commissioned the fresco went to Michelangelo when it was finished to complain that Raphael had overcharged him. But Michelangelo responded that "the knee alone is worth the price."

Just beneath the fresco with the "priceless knee" is a sculpture of Mary, Saint Anne and the Child Jesus completed by Andrea Sansovino in 1512. I have always thought that the sculpture was beautiful and charming. A friend made me aware of another dimension of the statue I had overlooked. Saint Anne is tickling the feet of her grandson, the child Jesus! And her smile of delight, in turn, brings a smile to all who notice it, and rejoice that indeed the saints are not so different from all of us. So there, with a smile, I pray for our grandparents and for all of our family members who bring to us a measure of ticklish delight at the wonder that is our life together.

It's A Small World

It is said that all roads lead to Rome. And that seemed to be true today as an exceptionally large crowd of people from all over the world gathered in Saint Peter's Square for the praying of the Angelus and the Sunday noon blessing of the Holy Father. Perhaps the beautiful sunny day with temperatures in the mid-50's proved inviting as people stood in the sunlight and listened to the words of Pope Benedict.

There I met Father Steven Masinde, an Apostle of Jesus from Uganda and cousin of Father Fred Wangwe, the parochial vicar at Saint Joseph in Mechanicsburg. Father Steven is studying in Rome. We had arranged to meet so that I could deliver a letter from Father Fred. And over lunch at a Chinese restaurant (a new experience for me in Rome!) I shared with him what I was doing on sabbatical and he shared with me the study he is doing for his thesis. He is researching "sacrifice" in the African tradition and how the Christian theology of the sacrifice of Jesus on the cross might "translate" into that African understanding. It was a pleasant meeting with stimulating conversation with a priest from Africa who has ties with someone back home. It is a small world!

Yesterday I visited a small religious shop next to my hotel. The owner of the shop asked me where I was from, and when I said: "the Harrisburg area," he replied: "Harrisburg? It's a beautiful day in Pennsylvania! Pete Wambach!" It seems he had met Mr. Wambach some time ago and knew of his fame as an historian and ambassador for Pennsylvania. It is a small world!

In his address at the noon blessing, Pope Benedict spoke of Saint Thomas Aquinas whose feast day is today. He spoke of the importance of dialogue between faith and reason, a topic close to the heart of the Holy Father. He said that faith need not fear reason and science, and science and reason need not fear faith. Calling to mind his address at the University of Regensburg during his recent visit to Germany, he expressed concern that, too often, science and reason reduce the world to the material, to what can be proven in a laboratory. When that happens the spirit languishes and humanity becomes impoverished. He also spoke of how Saint Thomas was in dialogue with the Jewish and Arab thinkers of his day and how that exchange enriched Aquinas's thinking and understanding of the human person. His words were timely and challenging.

Pope Benedict, with great passion, also expressed concern over the escalating violence in Lebanon and Gaza. He again spoke of the need for dialogue so that people who have lived with conflict and war for so long are able to find a way to peace together. I was reminded of the Pope's election and his choice of the name "Benedict." Early in the 20th century Pope Benedict XV tried lead the nations of the world to peace during the First World War. His words often fell on deaf ears. It seems that Pope Benedict XVI is also trying to be a voice of calm and reason in the midst of so much violence and hatred. I can only hope that those who guide the course of world events were listening to the impassioned plea of the Holy Father for dialogue, not warfare, as the way to a just and lasting peace.

From his window the Holy Father also released two doves and said that they were symbols of peace. He reminded us that we, too, are called to be signs of peace to the world.

Buona Domenica a tutti. A good Sunday to all.

Grocery Shopping In Rome

As you probably have figured out by now, I have many favorite places in Rome. And high on the list is the Campo Dei Fiori in the morning hours when the square is an open food market. I often used to walk through the market on the way to school back in the dark ages! And now when I visit Rome it is one of the places I return to often.

The square is properly named for as you enter there are several flower stands. No matter what the time of year there is a variety sure to please everyone's taste. At the center of the square is a statue of Giordano Bruno, a heretic who was burned on this spot during the Inquisition of 1600, not the church's finest hour I might add. I have a friend who calls the statue "Darth Vader." I rather like that. A little denial of history makes it less embarrassing for this cleric to walk through the square!

There are supermarkets in parts of Rome but they are nothing like the ones in America with aisles that seem to go on for miles. In some neighborhoods, like the Borgo area, shoppers rely on smaller grocery stores. One grocer near my hotel displays fruits and vegetables with such pride it looks like he is preparing a still life arrangement for an artist to paint. And if you are lucky, you live near an open market like the Campo dei Fiori, where each day you can shop and select the finest and freshest the sellers have to offer.

When Italians shop for groceries they do not go with a list. Rather, they go to the market to see what is available and then decide what dinner will be. "The artichokes look wonderful today, give me three. Is the swordfish fresh? Yes, it looks good. I'll have some. And lemons too." There is wisdom in all of this that goes beyond food shopping. And that wisdom might have something to say about how we approach life.

When I go to a grocery store with a list, I know what I want and I am determined to have it. I suppose there is nothing wrong with that. But if I am intent on apples and green beans it might mean that I am missing out on the first strawberries of the season or eggplants that radiate a purple freshness in the midmorning sun.

At times I think the greatest disappointments I experience in life come from living with a list of "wants" and "have to haves." And when life doesn't meet my expectations, I feel cheated, left out, put upon. Oh yes, I know that sometimes the list is necessary. I do have to have goals and objectives and dreams and hopes. But if I am so tied to what I want to accomplish, and to when and how I plan to do it, I might be missing out on a better or more promising possibility that comes my way simply by looking at what today is offering me, rather than at what I am expecting it to give.

"Surprise" is not a word we use often in the spiritual life. But perhaps we should. If I believe that the Spirit of God blows where it will, then I have to be ready to open my sails and go where the Spirit takes me today. And that destination, when it is Spirit-lead, will always have more to offer than the itinerary I had planned so carefully. Today, I might be thinking red sauce for dinner. But when I get to the market and there is a full bunch of fresh basil glistering in the sunlight, I had better make it pesto! Buon appetito!

Good Neighbors

It is hard not to be impressed by Saint Peter's Basilica. Words fall short of describing its beauty and its size. And to think that the Basilica is built over the tomb of the apostle Peter adds to the wonder and awe that a visitor experiences in considering the history and significance of this, the largest church in all of Christendom.

There is currently an exhibit in the "Charlemagne Gallery" commemorating the 500th anniversary of the laying of the foundation stone by Pope Julius II, upon which the basilica would be built. The exhibit includes architectural drawings, letters to and from Popes, manuscripts signed by Michelangelo, and paintings by Titian and Caravaggio, all recording in careful detail the history of the building of the Basilica.

At the very last gallery there is a curious and, I must say, an unexpected display. Shown in a glass case is the tattered robe that Saint Francis of Assisi wore when he came to Rome to receive permission from Pope Innocent III for the establishment of his order. When Francis came to Rome in the 12th century he sat among the beggars at the entrance of the first Saint Peter's, built by the Emperor Constantine in the fourth century. Also displayed is a letter written to Pope Pius XII by Mother Theresa asking permission to leave her religious community and found a new order to work with the poorest of the poor in Calcutta.

The display is a reminder that as magnificent as the Basilica of Saint Peters is, the church is about being the presence of Christ to others, especially the poor and outcast. And certainly there is no one in the history of Christianity who has personified that presence better than Saint Francis of Assisi in the 12th century, and Blessed Mother Theresa of Calcutta in the 20th century.

Appropriately enough, walking from the exhibit and turning right, behind a simple doorway is the Casa Dono di Maria (the gift of Mary), a soup kitchen staffed by the Missionaries of Charity, Mother Theresa's sisters. It is as if Saint Francis continues to sit among the poor in the shadows of Saint Peter's in the person of the Missionaries of Charity over 700 years later.

It is probably true that most visitors to Saint Peter's have no idea that the Casa Dono di Maria is there. But what is important is that those men and women who hunger for bread know that it is there, as the words of Jesus, "I was hungry and you gave me to eat" continue to be lived among those who are His followers, the living stones of His church.

A Day Without Joseph

Today, February 2, is the feast of the Presentation of the Lord. It is an ancient feast that recalls Joseph and Mary taking the child Jesus, their first born, to present him in the Temple and to offer a sacrifice "in accord with the dictate in the law of the Lord." The story, recorded in the second chapter of the Gospel of Luke, is filled with words and images that provide enough material for a lifetime of meditation.

I went to Mass this morning at the parish church of Saint Anne in Vatican City. Sort of. I went at 7:45 to pray Morning Prayer before the 8:00 Mass, only to discover that the priest who was celebrating the 7:00 Mass must have been long-winded! Because when I got there he was just beginning the Offertory! What's a fellow to do? So I went to Mass in reverse, celebrating the Liturgy of the Eucharist at the 7:00 Mass and then celebrating the Liturgy of the Word at the 8:00 Mass! Does it still count? I suppose the Lord understands!

At the 8:00 Mass the celebrant preached on Mary's faithfulness in bringing Jesus to the temple, and her obedience to the Law of the Lord. Excuse me! The gospel I heard said that "Mary AND Joseph took Jesus up to Jerusalem to present him to the Lord." But Joseph was nowhere to be found in that homily. I suppose it was just a case of the pastor of Saint Joseph Parish in Mechanicsburg being a little protective of his patron! That is one of the pitfalls of sitting on the other side of the pulpit! It is too easy to think: I would have said it differently!

Later that morning I decided to visit the church of Saint Frances of Rome in the Forum. Saint Frances is much loved by the Roman people. I had never been to that church and had wanted to visit if for some time. So I climbed up steps and down steps and up hills and down hills trying to find the entrance, only to discover that it is closed for restoration!

Someone once asked me how many churches there are in Rome. I have never been able to verify this but I was told that there are 400! If you have been to Rome you might believe it. It is like banks on Simpson Ferry Road in Mechanicsburg – there is one every 100 yards or so! The other day I listed all the churches in Rome I have visited over the years and came up with 72! So I decided I would try to make it an even 100 while I am here! A friend of mine told me that was too easy. That might be true but getting into some of these places (like Saint Frances of Rome) is no walk in the park. Especially since most of them close for siesta. Really! By the way I am up to 85!

Since Saint Frances didn't work out I did some exploring around the Forum. Then I discovered that the Church of Saints Luke and Martina at the other end of the Forum was opened and I had never been there before! So chalk up another church! By the way, there is a very interesting painting over the main altar of Saint Luke painting the Virgin Mary. One early tradition says that Luke was an artist and that he did paint a picture the Blessed Mother.

Still a little upset about Joseph being left in the shadows today I decided to visit the Church of Saint Joseph also located at the edge of the Forum. It was built over the Mamertine prison where tradition says Saints Peter and Paul were imprisoned before their martyrdom. I went to the prison, and then, you guessed it; the Church of Saint Joseph was closed! And it wasn't even siesta time yet! I asked the attendant at the prison when the church of Saint Joseph would be open. Would you believe, "the second and the fourth Sunday of the month until 11:30 a.m."? It sure has not been a good day for Saint Joseph.

Later in the afternoon I went for a walk to the Piazza Navona. I knew that on a back street along the way there is a church I had not visited, the Church of San Salvatore in Lauro. Yes, I know I am being a little obsessive about this visiting 100 churches thing! Well, siesta was over and even though it was not the second or fourth Sunday of the month, the church was open! Number 85!

And not only that, while I was sitting in the back (I got there in the middle of Benediction) I looked to the little chapel on my left and there was a 1731 painting by Pierleone Ghezzi of Saint Joseph with Saints Joachim and Anne, the parents of Mary! ALLELUIA! No cute little angels, no popes or cardinals hiding in the corner of the painting. Just Saint Joseph and his in-laws! Pierleone Ghezzi in church number 85 made my day! I could not take a picture since the chapel was dark but I did buy a cartolina and photographed it for the blog. It might sound a little irreverent but I cannot not help thinking that Joachim and Anne seem to be saying "Did you have to send her someone so old?"

In any case, Joseph did get his due today, at least in the parish Church of San Salvatore in Lauro, if not in the Vatican parish Church of St. Anne. And I will rest better tonight knowing that he did.

Thinking About The Church

"How do you get to Carnegie Hall?" the old joke asks. "Practice," of course, is the answer! "How do you get to Saint Peter's in Rome?" Well, actually there are two ways.

Most visitors approach the Basilica on the Via della Conciliazione, a broad avenue running from the Tiber River to the Piazza San Pietro. It is lined with palm trees and lanterns and "palazzi," some dating from the 16th century. All along the way the magnificent dome of Michelangelo is visible and there is a heightened sense that you are about to arrive at someplace very special, almost beyond this world. And someplace special it is indeed!

The other route (the way I take most visitors) is by way of the side streets surrounding Saint Peter's (the area called the Borgo) entering the Square through the Bernini colonnades encircling the piazza. Suddenly Saint Peter's is before you, catching the first-time visitor off guard. And that is how the Basilica and Piazza were designed to be seen some 500 years ago.

For you see, the Via della Conciliazione was only constructed in 1937. Prior to that time visitors winded their way through the streets of the Borgo and came upon Saint Peter's almost by surprise. But as a part of his Fascist urban planning, Benito Mussolini razed two streets of the Borgo and all of the buildings between them. And the approach to Saint Peter's Square became a monumental thoroughfare, more suited to the arrival of a visiting dignitary than the pilgrim who comes to the Basilica from the routine of everyday life seeking a place of refuge, a place of peace.

For me, it all comes down to ecclesiology, how we think about the Church. Bernini designed the two semi-circular colonnades as an extension of the Basilica in the mid 1600's. The effect is that of a mother's embrace, offering the visitor a place of welcome, a place of rest. "Leave the everyday world behind," the marble columns seem to say, "and find here, in this place, in this church, your Father's house." And so no matter what our day or lot in life has been, we are where we belong, embraced by God through the arms of His church.

All of that is lost for me when I walk the Via della Concilizaione. Its grandeur expects me to be more than I am. And in that expectation I lose the sense of Saint Peter's being a place of welcome. The Square is massive, some 790 feet wide, but by entering through colonnade its perfect proportions embrace, rather than dwarf me. Entry head-on along the regal Mussolini boulevard directs my gaze to Michelangelo's dome and the colonnades are lost somewhere in my peripheral vision. I am no longer embraced; I am swallowed up in the majesty of the place. It is no longer my Father's house where I am welcome; rather the church becomes a royal palace where only the worthy may enter.

Michelangelo knew when he designed his dome that it would not be seen as you approached the church. But he also knew that the dome of a church is a reminder of heaven. And heaven is for the life which is to come. So an uncluttered view is not my expectation. Something must be left for the world which is to come.

The month I have been in Rome has provided me with an opportunity to think about many things, and you can not be in Rome without thinking about the Church. Its history is written on every stone and its story is told in every corner of the city founded by the exploits of Romulus and Remus, but made holy by the blood of Peter and Paul. I have been thinking about how we, the living stones, present our church to the world. Are we a community that welcomes those who come to us from the side streets of life, often battered and shaken by the disappointments and fears that bracket their days? Or are we open only to those who heads are held high, the self-assured and the worthy?

How we answer this question will determine how we run our dioceses, how we structure our parishes, how we celebrate our liturgies, and most importantly, how we treat the most vulnerable in our community and in our world.

When I was a campus minister we celebrated our college Masses at the local parish church. One Sunday before Mass a parishioner who was joining us came to me and said "Father, you see that young man kneeling up there? I want you to go tell him to take off his baseball cap. He is in church." I thought for a moment and then said to the well-intentioned man, "I can't do that. If he removes his baseball cap, I am concerned that God will not recognize him. You see, he wears it all the time."

We come to the Church as we are. That is how God knows us. Not as we ought to be. Not as we think we should be. But as we are. And if the arms of God are willing to embrace us as we are, can we do less with others who seem to be sliding in by the side entrance, without name or title, even sometimes without vision or virtue?

Most mornings at Saint Peter's Square a man arrives who looks more like he is ready for the Mummer's parade than for a visit to Church. He kneels on the cobblestones and waves his arms, singing to the saints and preaching to the Pope. And yet no one seems to notice. He blends into the scenery as pilgrims make their way to the Basilica and Monsignori make their way to one of a hundred Vatican offices. He has found a welcome here in the shadow of Michelangelo's dome and the embrace of the Bernini colonnades. Somehow that is what I think our Father expects.

Thinking About Lent, Sin, Guilt And Shame

Yesterday I visited the Vatican Bookstore in Saint Peter's Square and noticed that Pope Benedict XVI had published his Lenten Message for 2007. Wanting to follow his good example I decided to publish my own Lenten message this year! Actually what follows are some ideas that have been seeking expression for some time. The leisure of sabbatical has given me the time to put those thoughts on paper.

Lent always has a way of creeping up on me. In the back of my mind I know that it is on its way, but somehow it seems to sneak in the back door. Just when I thought I had weeks to go, suddenly there it is before me. I know, of course, it is all about denial. If I don't think about it, maybe Lent will just disappear for this year! And yet it never does. My hoping that it will go away is probably proof that I need Lent!

This year is different for me. If I were at home I would be thinking about getting the parish ready for our Lenten observance. Do we have enough ashes? Has the purple drapery been ironed? Did we remember to put the schedule for Stations of the Cross in the bulletin? Have we ordered the palm and the Paschal Candle? I don't have to think about those things this year. Actually I did all that before I left! So this year I am able to think less about the external details associated with the observance of Lent and to focus a little bit more on the internal renewal to which the season calls us.

And what I find myself thinking about is sin! Actually, how we as a church think about and talk about sin. I have observed that in many of the things I have been reading and in many of the homilies I have heard since coming here, sin is a big topic! Again, it is my observation only and not a scientific study, but I find that the word that goes most often with sin is "guilt." And quite frankly it has been bothering me.

I went back and reread the Genesis story of Adam and Eve. You know the one. Eve forces Adam to eat the apple. Just kidding! But what I noticed is that when Adam and Eve do disobey God and eat the fruit of the tree in the middle of the garden ("apple" is never mentioned!), what they experienced was not "guilt" but "shame" as they covered themselves with fig leaves. Guilt is never mentioned. Does any work of art better show the shame of Adam and Eve as they leave the garden than Michelangelo's rendering on the ceiling of the Sistine Chapel?

I wonder why our focus has always been guilt. I am beginning to think it has something to do with power.

Guilt is experienced as a feeling. But like all feelings I have to decide which ones to trust and which ones to ignore. Sometimes I might "feel" guilty, but I might not be guilty of anything. For example, if I tell a friend I will meet him for dinner at 6:00 and get caught in traffic and do not have a cell phone, I might leave him waiting in the restaurant for an hour. I might "feel" guilty about that. But I am not guilty of anything except getting caught in a traffic jam!

The feeling of guilt is like the light on your dashboard that goes on warning you that there might be a problem with your engine; better have it checked. When I feel guilt about something, I have to open the hood and take a look and ask the question: "Have I done something wrong?" If not, I then make a conscious choice not to trust the feeling. But if indeed I have done something wrong, then I need to decide on a course of action to right the wrong, seek forgiveness, change direction or do whatever is appropriate in that situation.

The problem that I have with our emphasis on guilt is that it gets me nowhere. When guilt becomes the overriding feeling associated with my sin, all it does is say over and over again "you did something wrong, you messed up, you blew it!" Rather than becoming a warning sign to lead me to judgment and a course of action, guilt leaves me floundering in my inadequacies, in my mistakes, in my sin. It is as if I keep staring at the warning sign on the dashboard but never do anything to see first, if there is a problem, and then if there is, to try to correct it.

And here is where the issue of power enters in. If I can make people feel guilty (whether or not they are) then I render them powerless. By emphasizing their guilt, I shove them in a corner to contemplate how bad they are, and that gives me power over them. I become their prosecuting attorney, judge and jury rather than trusting them to take an inventory of their life situation and proceed appropriately.

And conversely, if I allow an individual, an institution, or an ideology to make me feel guilty then I have given them a power that is not theirs. If I allow myself to be drawn into a corner where I am left to contemplate how bad I am, then I have sold my birthright, which allows me as a child of God to live with dignity even if I have failed, even if I have sinned.

This is where my conscience enters in. Conscience is not a storehouse of rights and wrongs that I go to in order to see if what I have done is good or evil. Conscience is really more a verb than a noun. It is the decision-making ability that God has given to me to look at my actions, to carefully consider the gospel standards that I am called to in baptism, and then render a judgment on my guilt or innocence. Conscience is hard work! It demands honesty and careful thought. Sometimes it calls for consultation with a trusted friend or mentor, what the church calls a competent authority. And always it demands a willingness to be who I am, first to myself; then to God; and finally to others.

I would like to suggest that we put guilt in the "time-out corner" for awhile. And let's go back to the Genesis story and think about shame. There is a big difference between the two and that difference can determine whether I live a childish (not child-like) faith, or a mature faith.

Adam and Eve felt shame because they were not true to themselves, to the people God had created them to be. They ate of the tree of the knowledge of good and evil so that they could become like God. Being made in God's image and likeness was not enough for them. And when they had to face God they tried the good old "the devil made me do it" excuse. When that didn't fly and they were finally honest with themselves and then honest with God, they felt shame. It wasn't about the apple! It was about not living up to their dignity as children of God, having been made in His image and likeness.

If I sin and live in my guilt, I make no progress; that is where I remain. I get stuck in the "I am such a terrible person" mode and keep listening to the voices around me and in my own head that confirm my status as the lowest of the low. But when I feel shame it reminds me of who I really am, my true self. And then I begin to understand that I may have done something bad, but I am not bad. I may have sinned, but sinner is not my true identity. My identity is Child of God.

I think that is what happened to the Prodigal Son. When he left his father and squandered his inheritance it was not only his money that he lost. It was his identity as his father's son. His real hunger was not for bread; it was for the very soul that he left behind when he ran away from his father's estate. It was not guilt that led him home, it was shame. "Father, I have sinned against heaven and before you. I am no longer worthy to be called your Son."

During Lent the Church calls me to prayer, fasting and works of charity. Prayer invites me to take my place before the Father in heaven; the same Father who knew me before he formed me in my mother's womb (Psalm 139). Fasting challenges me to feed myself with only those things that foster health of body, mind and spirit. Works of charity empty my heart of love only that it might be filled with even greater love by the Father who rejoices that all his children live as one. Prayer, fasting and almsgiving are works of real repentance because they call me back to my true self; the self that is beloved by the Father.

On Ash Wednesday I am going to join the Church in praying Psalm 51: *Have mercy on me, O God, in your goodness; in the greatness of your compassion wipe out my offense. Thoroughly wash me from my guilt and of my sin cleanse me.*" And I am going to believe that the Lord does free me from my guilt as he calls me back to reclaim my birthright. And then I will pray the words of Psalm 34: *I sought the Lord, and he answered me, and delivered me from all my fears. Look to him and be radiant; so your faces shall never be ashamed.*

There is something about the way we are put together as human beings that needs signs and symbols to express the profound truths and unseen realities that are a part of our life of faith. We are "sacramental" by nature. We need "outward signs of inward grace."

On one of my first days in Rome I visited the Church of Saints Cosmas and Damian in the Roman Forum. It is cared for by the Franciscans of the Third Order Regular. The Friars have placed a beautiful sculpture of Saint Francis at the entrance of the Church. It stands against the ruins of the Basilica of Constantine. Francis' arm lifted to the heavens, with the ruins of the old order in the background, illustrates what I have been trying to say about God's amazing grace moving me beyond guilt and shame. The sculpture reminds me of the words we sing in the hymn adapted from Beethoven's *Ode to Joy:* "Child of God lift up thy head."

This Lent, may we lift up our heads, not in pride; but in humble gratitude for the dignity that is ours as children of God. Through the death and rising of Jesus, we are invited to live not in fear and guilt and shame. Rather we live as those forgiven and beloved by the Father.

Lent On The Aventine Hill

You might say that Lent in officially begins in Rome on the Aventine, one of the original seven hills of the Eternal City. On Ash Wednesday afternoon Pope Benedict XVI will lead cardinals, archbishops, and bishops in a penitential procession from the Church of San Anselmo to the Church of Santa Sabina. Joining them will be the Benedictine Monks of San Anselmo and the Dominican Priests of Santa Sabina. At Santa Sabina the Holy Father will celebrate Mass and impose ashes to mark the beginning of the Penitential Season.

Following an ancient tradition, Santa Sabina is the designated "Station Church" for Ash Wednesday. Each day of Lent a church in Rome is marked as the station church for that particular day. On those days the faithful make a pilgrimage to the church for prayer during this holy season. Many of these historic churches were once "house churches," where during times of persecution the early Christians gathered for prayer and the celebration of the Eucharist.

Santa Sabina was built in the fifth century over the house of the Roman matron Sabina. Excavations under the church have unearthed a Roman house from the third century. On the rear wall a mosaic announces that the church was erected by the priest Peter of Illyria during the reign of Pope Celestine I. It was restored in the 9th century and again in the late 16th century and once more in the early 20th century. But the church, as it is today, is essentially the church of the fifth century Christians.

It is a perfect example of the early basilica style. The columns in the nave are from an ancient Roman temple on the Aventine that was dedicated to either Diana or Juno.

In 1219 the church was entrusted to the care of Saint Dominic. The Dominicans continue to care for Santa Sabina. The cell of Saint Dominic is in the Dominican convent next to the church and is open to visitors.

Praying The Psalms

Much of what I have been sharing has been related to places I visited while in Rome. In addition to visiting churches and historic sites, I have also been reading about the Psalms. For some time I have wanted to study these ancient "prayer-poems" that play such an important role in our liturgy, our public prayer together, and also in the praying of the Divine Office or Liturgy of the Hours.

In my seminary studies I was blessed with courses in Sacred Scripture that continue to guide and inspire me today, especially in preparation for preaching. However, for some reason I have no recollection of the time I spent studying the Psalms. That has always puzzled me because the professor who taught the course was very good. I do remember other courses he taught but not the course on the Psalms. I think my present study has shed some light on the reason.

The Psalms are filled with great emotion. The writers who composed them and the community that prayed them were not afraid to have their hearts speak directly to the Lord God, Yahweh. The Psalms speak of the joys and blessings as well as the pain and despair of God's chosen people.

Psalm 137 tells of the anguish of the Jewish people when they were taken into captivity in Babylon after the destruction of the Temple and the city of Jerusalem. *"By the rivers of Babylon, we sat mourning and weeping when we remembered Zion,"* cries the Psalmist. *"On the poplars of that land we hung up our harps... How can we sing a song of the Lord n a foreign land?"*

On the other hand, Psalm 126 speaks of the joy of return when the captivity was ended. *"When the Lord restored the fortunes of Zion, then we thought we were dreaming. Our mouths were filled with laughter; our tongues sang for joy..."*

At times there will be a change of mood within the same Psalm, moving from great despair to great hope within a few verses. Psalm 69, a Psalm of David, is a good example. The prayer begins with a tale of desperation. *"Save me, O God! For the waters have reached my neck. I have sunk into the mire of the deep, where there is no foothold; I have gone down to the watery depths; the flood overwhelms me. I am weary with my crying and my throat is parched."* But by the end of the prayer the Psalmist proclaims: *"But I am afflicted and in pain; let your saving help protect me, God, that I may praise God's name in song and glorify it with thanksgiving."*

After study and reflection, I think I understand the reason my seminary study of the Psalms left little impression. I was 23 or 24 years old at the time. Life was carefree, filled with promise and revolved around me and the other seminarians who shared it. In short, I lacked the life experience necessary to understand the mind and heart of the Psalmist. What did I know of "deep waters" sweeping over me or a throat that is "parched" from weariness and crying? It is no wonder the study left my mind; there was not an empty place in my heart to give it rest.

But now, some thirty years later, with life experience of my own and life experience shared with others through my ministry, I am better able to understand and identify with the Psalmist who cries out to God in joy and in sorrow. The range of life's emotions I have known and have shared with others invites me to find a meeting place with the Psalmist – a common ground where we are able to speak the same language, the language of the human heart.

To be able to pray the Psalms I need to remember that the Psalmist is just like me. I have to recognize in the Psalms the same emotions, the same fears and the same frustrations, joys and hopes that I have known in my own life. My time and circumstance in history may be different, but on the level of the human heart my experience of life is the same as King David's in Psalm 63, when he prayed in fear for his life in the wilderness of Judah; and is the same experience as the unknown author of Psalm 113 whose lips are filled with praise for the Lord "*who raises the needy from the dust, and lifts the poor from the ash heap.*"

To pray the Psalms I need to try to understand not only the mind and heart of the people who wrote and prayed them so long ago, but I also have to know my own mind and heart as well. The challenge of praying the Psalms is to bring my world and the world of the Psalmist together. So when my day is bright and filled with promise but the Psalmist speaks of "terror on every side," I am challenged to join him at that place in my heart when on another day I, too, had known his fear. Likewise, when my life seems empty and routine while the Psalmist is rejoicing in "the wonderful works the Lord has done," I am asked to move from the emptiness of my routine and remember along with the Psalmist the blessings that life at another moment had offered to me.

I believe that when we pray we never pray alone. We are always joined with the Communion of Saints and with all of those who have gone before us in life and faith. Praying the Psalms makes that recognition real as I enter into the experience of God's chosen people in a time long ago in a place far away. But in the mystery of prayer the distance of time and place fade into the background and there is only the present moment when all of God's beloved pray together before His throne.

A Valentine Day Pilgrimage

Today is Valentine's Day and the feast of Saints Cyril and Methodius. So I went to the Basilica of San Clemente to place flowers at the tomb of Saint Cyril and to pray for the three Sisters who faithfully serve our parish of Saint Joseph in Mechanicsburg on this, their feast day.

I prayed in thanksgiving for Sister Agnes Marie, Sister Joseph Therese and Sister Michael Ann and the many ways they share faith with the children of our parish. While lighting three candles in the chapel where Cyril is buried I also prayed for all of the Sisters of their community whose Motherhouse is in Danville, Pennsylvania.

Cyril and Methodius were brothers who preached the Gospel in Moravia in the 9th century. They translated the Gospels and liturgical texts into the old Slavic language using what would later be known as the Cyrillic alphabet. Cyril came to Rome from Crimea in 868 and brought with him the remains of Pope Clement to be buried underneath the altar of the basilica dedicated to the fourth Pope. He died in Rome on this day in 869 and was buried in the Church of San Clemente. His brother Methodius became a bishop and died on April 6, 885 in Velebrad in the Czech Republic. Together with Saint Benedict, they are the patrons of Europe.

The Body of Saint Cyril was found beneath the present basilica in the original church built in the fourth century. Today that place is marked by a simple altar and a mosaic of the Saint. His body was moved to the upper church and buried under an altar in a side chapel dedicated to the two brothers. The painting behind the altar shows Cyril and Methodius with Pope Hadrian II, who is handing a replica of the church to Christ. Recent excavations of the lower church have found an ancient fresco that matches a description of the burial of Saint Cyril. Now archeologists and scholars think this new site may have been his first grave.

The present Basilica of San Clemente is built over the original fourth century church, which, in turn, is built over a public building of Imperial Rome that was destroyed in the fire of Nero in 64 A.D. That building contained a Mithraic chapel. Both the original church and lower level Roman building are open to the public. The long history of the site is too complex to try to describe in a short narrative. But something should be said about the wonderful 12th century apse mosaic in the upper church.

It depicts the cross of Christ with Mary and Saint John on either side. The apostles are represented by 12 doves that rest on the cross. Living waters flow from the cross (the tree of life) and provide nourishment to an acanthus bush below. Branches and leaves fill the apse and swirl about its surface. In its embrace are found people, animals, birds and flowers, all receiving sustenance from the living waters of the cross. All of creation and all of humanity are pictured, from the most simple (a peasant woman feeding her chickens) to the most powerful (the pagan gods Jupiter and Neptune riding a dolphin).

At the top of the mosaic the hand of God the Father extends from the heavens and presents a crown of victory for his son. The Basilica and its apse mosaic are a wonderful valentine for all who visit this holy place and are reminded of the redemptive love of our God manifested in the sacrifice of his Son, Jesus. Visiting the church on the Feast of Saints Cyril and Methodius and praying at the tomb of Cyril, made it a day of special blessing for me. Happy Feast Day, Sisters!

Saint Peter In Rome

February 22 is the Feast of the Chair of Peter. It is a celebration of the authority that Jesus entrusted to Saint Peter when he said to him: *"You are Peter, and upon this rock I will build my church, and the gates of the nether world shall not prevail against it. I will give you the keys to the kingdom of heaven. Whatever you bind on earth shall be bound in heaven; and whatever you loose on earth shall be loosed in heaven."* (Matthew 16:18-19)

Peter was martyred in Rome in the first century in the Circus of Nero and buried in a nearby pagan cemetery. In the fourth century, Constantine built the first Saint Peter's Basilica over Peter's tomb. In the 16th century Pope Julius tore down that church and began construction of the church that stands today. Within the basilica there are two monuments which celebrated Peter's authority.

The Chair of Saint Peter, in the apse of the basilica, was designed by Gian Lorenzo Bernini in the 17th century. One tradition says that when Peter came to Rome he received hospitality at the home of the Roman Senator Pudens. Today the Church of San Pudenziana is built over his home. A chair from that house is said to have been Peter's Episcopal throne or chair ("cathedra" in Latin). That chair is enclosed with the ebony and bronze throne of the Bernini monument. On either side of the chair are statues of two eastern and two western Doctors of the Church: Anselm, Athanasius, John Chrysostem and Augustine. Above the monument is the window of the Holy Spirit, also designed by Bernini.

Also in the Basilica is a bronze statue of Peter seated on a throne. Recent restoration suggests that the statue was designed by Arnolfo di Cambio. It was placed in its present location to celebrate the 25th anniversary of the election of Pope Pius IX, the longest reigning Pope.

The right foot of Saint Peter on the statue has been worn smooth by the touch and kisses of pilgrims. On special feast days the statue is dressed in liturgical vestments.

In addition to the tradition that says that Peter lived with the Senator Pudens, there are some who hold that he would have stayed with the Jewish community in Rome who were living in the Trastevere section of the city at that time. There has been a Jewish community in Rome since long before the time of Christ. At a later date they moved across the river near Tiber Island in what is called the "ghetto." There were times throughout the centuries when the Jewish community was restricted to life within the ghetto and forced to listen to sermons in a nearby church. Today the ghetto is home to the Synagogue of Rome. In his ongoing effort to promote understanding and respect among all peoples of faith, Pope John Paul II visited there and became the first Pope since Peter to visit a synagogue.

The ghetto is still home to a small Jewish community. There you will find shops and restaurants that are a part of the rich cultural heritage of the Roman Jews. During World War II some members of the Jewish community were imprisoned in Rome and some were killed in the Nazi concentration camps. There are many stories of Romans who sheltered Jews during the war. The tiny church of San Benedetto (Saint Benedict) in Trastevere was one of those places.

In Rome, Peter and Paul are always pictured together. Peter is a reminder to us of our spiritual ties to Judaism, and Paul is a reminder that the Gospel was also preached also to the Gentiles. On February 22 we celebrate Peter's authority and, in the spirit of Pope John Paul II, we pray for continued growth in understanding and respect between Christians and Jews.

Preparing To Leave Rome
The Broader Our Vision – The More We See Of God

When I am in Rome with family or friends, at the end of their stay I like to ask what has been the most significant experience of their visit. As I prepare to leave Rome next Monday I have been asking myself the same question: "In the past seven weeks, is there any experience that stands out above the others?"

It is a difficult question to answer. My time here has been restful; my reading and study have been intellectually stimulating; the time for prayer in so many beautiful churches has been of great spiritual benefit; and the history, art, architecture and culture of continue to fill me with awe and delight. Since there have been many significant moments during these past seven weeks, how could I choose just one? So I have decided to share with you several experiences that have made a lasting impression. I do that recognizing that with any meaningful travel, the blessings continue long after the trip is over. In the weeks, months and even years ahead I expect that there will be other things that will come to mind from my time in Rome that I will count as special blessings. For although I leave the Eternal City and move on to Jerusalem, I take the time spent here with me in heart, mind and memory.

One of the most memorable times was a visit to the Church of Saint Nicholas in Carcere, located next to the Theatre of Marcello between the Tiber River and the Palatine Hill. I may have been to this church before but I do not remember it. I read about it before visiting and knew that it was built upon the foundation of three ancient Roman temples of the third century B.C. The temples were dedicated to Janus, Juno Sospita and Spes.

As I started looking around the church a young man approached and asked if I spoke Italian. With some hesitation I answered "Yes, a little." He told me he was an official guide and would be happy to take me on a tour, including the area beneath the church if I would like to see the foundation of the ancient temples upon which San Nicolo was built. I was only too happy to agree and the tour began.

The guide was very knowledgeable and seemed pleased to be able to share his knowledge with someone, since it was a very slow day for visitors to San Nicolo. Much of the vocabulary of architecture and archeology is familiar to me from my study of art history. With that background and the illustrations, diagrams and charts provided along the way I was able to understand most of what the guide said.

What was most impressive to me was how the unknown architect incorporated one of the ancient temples into the design of this 11th century church. Not only are the columns of the central nave taken from one of the original temples, but the walls of the central temple were incorporated into the north and south external walls of the church. Built over an earlier sanctuary and remolded in 1599, this church was literally built into the structure of one of the earliest pagan temples.

The visit to San Nicolo was thrilling and reminded me of how often in the churches of the Eternal City there are traces of the civilization and culture of ancient Rome. I will cite a few examples.

The signs of the Zodiac are embedded in marble discs surrounding the obelisk in the center of Saint Peter's Square, following a practice common in the atrium of both private homes and public buildings in pagan Rome. In a Christian tomb in the ancient cemetery beneath Saint Peter's Basilica, a mosaic of Apollo (the sun god) racing across the heavens is used to represent Jesus, the Son of God rising from the dead and ascending to heaven at the right hand of the Father. On the ceiling of the Sistine Chapel, Michelangelo has Hebrew Prophets and Pagan Sibyls seated side by side framing the biblical scenes of Creation in the center of the ceiling. As mentioned in a previous entry, the apse mosaic in the Church of San Clemente shows the pagan gods Jupiter and Neptune swirling about the world redeemed by the life giving waters of the cross of Christ. I am also reminded that Saint Augustine used the philosophy of Plato and Saint Thomas Aquinas used the philosophy of Aristotle to develop their theologies that continue to influence our understanding of the Christian faith.

Everything that is a part of the created world, everything that is a part of the human experience has the potential to teach us something about our nature and God's plan for the salvation of the world. I think of the psalmist telling us in Psalm 19: *The heavens declare the glory of God; the sky proclaims its builders craft;* and of the poet Gerard Manley Hopkins boasting that *the world is charged with the grandeur of God.*

I am not so naïve that I see the world through rose-colored glasses, but I do believe, that with a discerning eye and informed judgment, we can trust the first lesson of the Bible: *God looked at everything he had made, and he found it very good.* (Genesis 1:31) There is much to be learned from the world that once was and the world that is around us today. Not all is bad; not all is harmful to the human spirit.

I think of people I have known who do not share my faith or, in some instances, who do not profess any faith, but who have been examples of generous love and compassion and show a commitment to the work of justice and peace for the well-being of the human community. I remember countless trips to museums around the world where I found inspiration and beauty in much of what might be termed "secular art." My reading of literature and history reminds me of how one civilization is invited to build upon the strengths of those who have gone before it, even if those civilizations differ greatly in philosophical, political or religious tradition.

It is interesting to me that in coming to Rome, a city that is the focal point of Western civilization and Catholic Christianity, my vision has expanded to see the possibility of learning truth in ways that may be very different from what is familiar and what I hold dear. When I step outside the circle of my experience I do not lose my balance, rather I gain a broader perspective from which to appreciate all that I have learned and all that I profess to be meaningful and true.

Michelangelo recognized, even in the pagan world, a genuine search for truth and so he was bold enough to place Pagan Sibyls alongside Hebrew Prophets on the Pope's ceiling. The builder of San Nicolo did not think it necessary to raze the pagan temples when he built the church; he saw, in the Christian dispensation, a way of bringing to fulfillment the pagan world's inner disposition toward the divine. When Gian Lorenzo Bernini included the signs of the Zodiac in the pavement of Saint Peter's Square, he recognized, in all times and seasons, a movement toward their Creator. The mosaicist who placed the gods Neptune and Jupiter in the apse above the high altar of San Clemente celebrated the mercy of God being powerful enough to embrace worlds beyond our imagining. And those responsible for the decoration of the Christian mausoleum near the tomb of the Apostle Peter saw the sun-god Apollo prefiguring the coming of the Son of God, inviting redeemed humanity to share eternal life with him in heaven.

The Second Vatican Council's document on the church in the modern world (*Gaudium et Spes*) reminds us that we do live "in the world." And in that world the hand of God is at work, continuing to mold, and form, and shape His creation into a thing of beauty, a work of art. We are challenged in our living to see that divine hand at work and to rejoice that we are a small part of the infinite plan of the Creator for the salvation of worlds far beyond our reach.

I have learned much in my time here. I have also come to appreciate, all the more, what I had learned before my visit, thanks to the educational opportunities I have had and the teachers who challenged me to see worlds beyond those that appear. Truth is a part of the mystery of who God is. Just as I cannot fully comprehend the mystery of God's being, so, too, I can never fully understand the majesty of truth that is a part of that mystery. Once I think I have captured (understood) God, God disappears leaving me to my own imaginings. In the same way, once I think I am able to fully understand (capture) truth, I am left alone with my awkward explanations of the mystery of it all.

The broader our vision, the more we see of God. The narrower our focus, the less of God there is to see. It is a rather modest 11th century church, built into the ruins an ancient pagan temple in the heart of old Rome, that has brought me to this important spiritual realization.

Preparing To Leave Rome
The Eternal City – A Feast For The Eyes

Rome is a feast for the eyes. At every step along the way, at each turn of the corner, at the top of stairways that seen to go on for miles, there is sensory overload. It might be the waters of a Renaissance fountain sparking in the morning sunlight; or the façade of a Baroque church, regal and majestic; or a pagan temple from the second century B.C. laughing in the face of time; or the noble faces of Roman men and women looking like the sculptures of their ancestors in the Vatican museum.

You cannot walk the streets of Rome and be passive before the layers of history and the panorama of beauty that greet you along the way. Even if you have seen it a hundred times before, each and every sight demands a response. At one moment it might be a knowing smile and the whispered words: "I know what that is!" At the next moment a perplexed look that wonders: "I've passed this way countless times. How could I not have noticed that before?" I've tripped over cobblestones too many times to count because I could not take my eyes off the sights unfolding before me. That is one of the things I like best about Rome.

In addition to living here for four years as a student, I have visited the Eternal City numerous times. And so I ask myself: "Why have I decided to spend so many weeks of my sabbatical in Rome when there are many other places I would like to visit?"

I suppose there are many answers to that question. Yes, Rome is a kind of homecoming for me. Yet when I come here it is not nostalgia for a time past that attracts me. Yes, Rome is familiar so it is easy feeling secure with little concern for language or getting lost. But it is not familiarity with place and custom that brings me back. And of course Rome is the center of the institutional church. But even that is not why I come here often and why I chose to be here for so long during this sabbatical.

I have decided that one of the major reasons I want to be here, whenever possible, is the pleasure I get in the visual richness of the urban Roman landscape. As I said in the opening sentence, Rome is a feast for the eyes. It is easy to be romantic about the city. Rome is also a nation's capital and a city of over three million people, and like any major city, it is not easy to live in. Traffic, crowds, traffic, graffiti, traffic, high prices, noise. And did I mention traffic???

But perhaps it is all of that that makes the spotting of an ancient column hiding behind a phalanx of motorcycles, or the sound of the neighborhood fountain gurgling between the blare of car horns, all the more intoxicating. A flower-laden window above the turmoil of the city is like an oasis in the desert. A 17th century Madonna on the corner building of a piazza where begging gypsies try to pickpocket unsuspecting tourists adds a feeling of calm and humanity to an otherwise uncomfortable situation. A Latin inscription from 49 A.D. announcing that Claudius, the "acclaimed emperor of the ninth tribunate" has declared this place to be the new expanded boundary of the city makes you forget the political graffiti marring the wall of the medieval palazzo next door. Even the sight of laundry hanging on an apartment balcony has a humanizing effect on the chaos of a city that, at times, seems less than friendly to residents and visitors alike.

A few Sundays ago I got up early to visit the church of Saint Joseph at the edge of the Imperial Forum. It is one of those churches that has strange visiting hours. It is only open in the morning of the second Sunday of the month; however like many sights in Rome, it was worth the inconvenience.

I like to remind visitors to the city that Rome is not some Disney World built for the enjoyment of tourists. It is a city where people raise families and go to work each day; where public officials try to govern a nation which, for centuries, has rejected attempts at being governed; where the cardinals, bishops, priests and sisters who work in the Vatican buy their groceries standing in line with the carpenter who lives next door. But unlike other cities, there are treasures whose history and beauty are not to be found anywhere else.

Where else can you find a third century statue tucked away in the corner of a busy piazza? Or how many cities boast the presence of Egyptian obelisks that were seen by Moses, Cleopatra, Julius Caesar and Saint Peter? Only in Rome can you visit a church that serves as the opening scene of an opera, and a fortress where the opera's heroine falls to her death in the last act. Only in Rome is a church called "new" even though it was built nearly 400 years ago. Where else, but in the eternal city, do vendors close their shops in midday, knowing that spending a few hours around the dining room table with family and friends is more important than making one more sale?

Why would I want to go anywhere else?

Preparing To Leave Rome
Dining As An Event

Dining in Rome is an event, but it is not all about the food; and it is not limited to a formal, sit-down meal at a restaurant. Let me share an experience I had just today that I would count among my most memorable during this stay in Rome.

Breakfast does not play a major role in Italian households. A quick espresso, maybe a roll with a little marmalade or a cornetto at the local bar, and then it's off to work or school. But midmorning there is a tradition of stopping by the local forno (bakery) or bar for "pizza bianca." Walk down any street about 10:30 A.M. and you will find blue collar workers and women in fur coats eating what is little more than baked pizza dough with just the right amount of salt and olive oil to make it irresistible. At the Panificio next to my hotel, Angelo will tell you that his is the best on the Borgo Pio because he makes it just like his family does in a little town not far from Assisi in Umbria. The secret, he tells me, is a little "rosmarino." He is right! A little rosemary does make all the difference.

This morning as I was walking down the street on the way to the internet café, I passed by a local pizzeria where you can buy pizza by the slice. I have been very good at resisting the "pizza bianca" tradition, preferring to save my carbs for pasta at lunch! But today I noticed that they had just taken a tray from the oven and I could not resist! After all, these are my final days in Rome and I am sure there will not be pizza bianca in Jerusalem!

When I went into the store the attendant was on his cell phone. He said to the person on the other end: "I must go. A man whose face is as bright as the sun has just entered the store!" There was a pause, and then he said to me: "My wife sends you kisses!" Would that happen in

America? When he finished his conversation he took me on a "tour" of each and every kind of pizza he had to offer. He offered samples to be sure I bought just what I wanted. There was, of course, traditional tomato and cheese pizza, called margherita in Italy, but with much lighter crust than we serve in America. There was his mother-in-law's specialty, pizza con quattro formaggio, pizza with four cheeses. And then he insisted that I try the pizza with red and green peppers! He was only too happy to spend time with me and proudly share the fruit of his labor.

Do you see what I mean; it's not all about the food?

Since I left Rome as a student thirty years ago there are definitely more "fast food" type restaurants in the city. There is even a McDonald's across the piazza from the Pantheon. I must say that I was happy to see that the Dunkin' Donuts at the Trevi Fountain had closed! Although more people seem to be eating on the run, the tradition of spending time at table with family or friends is still alive and well in Italy.

In Italy the job of waiter is a respected profession and almost always held by men. Most restaurants do not open until 12:30 or 1:00 in the afternoon. They serve "pranzo" until 3:00 or 3:30 and then close for siesta; they do not open again until 7:00 or 7:30. Arrive at 6:30 and you will see the staff sitting together enjoying their evening meal (cena) before they unlock the doors.

I do not know if there is any one way to adequately describe a "typical" Italian meal but it usually consists of several courses, ordered one at a time. As you make your way through each course, there is ample time for conversation and more wine. The table is yours for as long as you like. The check is not presented until you ask for it and, even then, it may take two or three requests. Waiters are happy to tell you about the daily specials (Thursday is "gnocchi day" in Rome) and to make suggestions. I have observed that many Italians do not look at a menu. They have a discussion with the waiter about their likes and dislikes and often follow his suggestions. Fish is always fresh and often on display in a case as you enter the restaurant. The same is true of the antipasto table. Vegetables like spinach or chicory or artichokes are usually served at room temperature. The pasta is always "al dente" and grated cheese is never served with any fish or seafood pasta! Ask for it with your spaghetti with clam sauce and the waiter will think you are pazzo (crazy). If you are a regular at a restaurant you might be treated to an after dinner drink like limoncello or grappa.

Dining in an Italian restaurant is like going to church! There is tradition, ritual and an understanding that what is really happening is more than the eye can see or words can describe. The food is important but what happens around the table is of equal worth.

Finding a restaurant you like in Rome is like making a new friend. In time the waiter knows what kind of wine you drink; if you like your mineral water "naturale" or "frizzante"; and he always wants to know how your day has been and where you plan to visit tomorrow.

One day early in my stay here I wandered into a "new" restaurant and was warmly greeted by one of the waiters. The service and food were excellent. When I returned two weeks later I was the first person in the restaurant. The same waiter greeted me; his face lit up and he said in all sincerity: "I am happy you came back. Sit down and be comfortable. There is something I want you to try." And before I knew it there was a bowl of lentil soup in front of me. "The chef just made it," he said. "Tell me if you think it is ok." OK? It was wonderful! I had found a good restaurant. I had made a new friend. I had been to church!

Preparing To Leave Rome
Some Final Thoughts About The Church

Very little is known about the time that Simon Peter spent in Rome; however we do know that he brought with him from Jerusalem his experience of the life, ministry, death and resurrection of Jesus. It was that message he preached with great fervor; and it was that preaching that led to his martyrdom in the Circus of Nero in 62 A.D. With Peter's arrival in Rome, the heart of the Church moved from Jerusalem to the Eternal City.

The first followers of Jesus in Rome were few in number; however, in the beginning of the fourth century as their numbers grew and the persecution of the Christians ended with the Edict of Constantine, the Church began to take on a decidedly Roman flavor. What began as a small sect within the Judaism of Palestine in the first half of the first century, in a short time became the Holy Roman Catholic Church.

The structure and language of the Roman Empire was adapted to fit the needs of the growing church. Even the first public places for Christian worship in the city were modeled after Roman law courts called basilicas. With religious as well as political authority the Emperor was called the Pontifex Maximus, the great high priest. The 17th century inscription on the façade of Saint Peter's Basilica notes that it was constructed by Pope "Paul V Borghese, the Roman High Priest." The earliest mosaics in the city show Peter dressed not in the grab of Palestine, but wearing a Roman toga.

I think of all of this as I prepare to leave for Jerusalem. In one sense I seem to be doing things backwards. Perhaps I should have followed Peter's lead and started in Jerusalem and moved on to Rome. Be that as it may, I leave with many images of the Church in Rome that attest to its longevity and its ability to withstand turmoil from without as well as from within.

This morning I paid a final visit to a favorite small chapel a few blocks from the Vatican. On one wall are the remains of a 16th century fresco. The painting shows Pope Gregory the Great, in the sixth century, praying before Castle San Angelo at a time when Rome was under siege by the barbarians and also suffering the devastating effects of the plague. Gregory had a vision of the Archangel Michael, standing above the castle with his fiery sword drawn. Through his intercessions the plague ended and the northern hordes turned back.

In front of the Basilica of Saint John Lateran, the Pope's Cathedral, there is a statue of Saint Francis of Assisi and his companions. Francis came to Rome in the 13th century to seek approval for his new order. The Pope had a dream that night that the Lateran basilica was crumbling, but Francis was holding it up. The Holy Father took that as a sign that the simple way of life espoused by the beggar from Assisi, had much to offer the Church and so he gave his approval to what was to become the Franciscan Order.

The challenges and problems we face in the church today are known by all of us. The sexual abuse of children by members of the clergy has brought devastating harm to victims and their families. The scandal of cover up and the failure to act by some members of the hierarchy has stirred the anger of the faithful and lessened the credibility of Church leaders. Even Pope John Paul II's granting a position of privilege in Rome to a deposed American Cardinal gives indication that perhaps the institutional Church still does not understand the harm that pedophile priests and bishops have wrought, and the disappointment and furor that lies just beneath the surface of those scandalized by bishops and cardinals whose failure to act makes them accessories to the crime.

We all know the worry and disappointment we experience when our children and family members no longer practice the faith we tried so hard to pass onto them as a way to a meaningful life. We wonder if we can ever find a way to show them that the Catholic experience has much to offer them for a meaningful existence in our often violent and misguided world.

The Second Vatican Council called us to be a force for good in the modern world. However, when confronted with the multitude and complexity of problems we face in our nation and the world today we wonder, as a people of faith, if we can even begin to make a difference when the values of so many seem to be far removed from all that we hold to be meaningful and true.

I noted previously that on February 22nd, the feast of the Chair of Peter, the bronze statue of Peter close to his tomb is dressed in a red liturgical cape and papal tiara. I went to Saint Peter's early that day and was one of the first visitors to the cathedral. I wanted to see the statue without a crowd of people around. It was impressive, regal and I was moved; but as a pastor and a fellow pilgrim along the way, I also came away with a few questions.

Has the structure of our Church become too top-heavy and layered with a bureaucracy that sometimes loses touch with the day-to-day struggles of God's people?

Do those who make decisions, in secret behind closed Vatican doors, have any idea of what the life of the everyday faithful Catholic is all about?

Have we equated the Gospel call to holiness with the obeying of rules, inadvertently creating the very kind of Pharisee-ism that Jesus could not abide?

Have we forgotten that the Gospel is intended to free people to live their dignity as children of God, made in His image and likeness; or do we create structures and rules that burden more than they liberate?

Do those structures and rules present an image of the Church to the world that is more the Empire of the Elect rather than the Kingdom of God?

Do we present the sacramental life of the Church as a way to holiness or have the sacraments become a gold star for good conduct or rewards for those who have already attained the heights of virtue?

Do we pay more attention to the rubrics that govern our rituals than we do to their spirit that gives life?

Do we believe that all the faithful receive the Holy Spirit in Baptism and Confirmation, or do we recognize the gifts of Wisdom, Understanding and Right Judgment in only those who hold decision-making authority by virtue of ordination?

I know there are some who will find these questions disturbing. There will be those who will question my loyalty to the Church and assume that I am espousing an ecclesiology that does not respect the authority of the Church. Yet nothing could be further from the truth; nothing could do more to misinterpret my motivation. It is precisely because the Church is at the center of my life that I have to acknowledge what might be obstacles to the living and preaching of the Gospel in our time and place in history.

I was reminded recently of a statement I had heard some years ago but have not thought about in quite some time. The Church does not have a mission; the mission has a Church. We all live in service to the mission entrusted to us by the Lord Jesus to go forth and preach the Gospel (good news) to all people. As I leave the city of Peter and travel to the city where it all began, I pray that our Church, all of us, will be faithful to that mission to share the Gospel with our world and with all who share our lives; a gospel prefigured in the preaching of Isaiah when he proclaimed: *Have you not known? Have you not heard? The Lord is the everlasting God, the Creator of the ends of the earth. He does not faint or grow weary, his understanding is unsearchable. He gives power to the faint, and to him who has no might he increases strength. Even youths shall faint and be weary, and young men shall fall exhausted; but those who wait for the Lord shall renew their strength, they shall mount up with wings like eagles, they shall run and not be weary, they shall walk and not faint. (Isaiah 40:28-31)*

Next week, Jerusalem! Shalom!

Jerusalem

Arriving In Jerusalem

I rejoiced when they said to me, "Let us go to the house of the Lord." And now our feet are standing within your gates, Jerusalem. Jerusalem, built as a city, walled round about. Here the tribes have come, the tribes of the Lord. (Psalm 122)

Riding in an airport shuttle from Tel Aviv to Jerusalem, on a rainy Monday afternoon, it is easy to understand what the Psalmist meant when he speaks of "going up" to Jerusalem. The forty-five minute ride from the coast to the Judean hills gives a sense, even on a foggy day, of the thrill that the early pilgrims must have felt as they saw the hills before them. The joy of seeing Jerusalem high above the others does indeed gladden the heart.

Among my first impressions: I had forgotten about how bad Jerusalem traffic is! When a young man in the shuttle questioned the driver about the traffic he said simply: "This city was built for camels and donkeys, not for cars. The important people, who make those decisions, sit around a table drinking all day and do nothing!" What a shame he was hesitant to voice an opinion to strangers! His frankness is one of the things I like about Israelis!

Because there was a light rain and also because dusk was near I thought I would simply unpack and relax. But when I looked out my window and saw the Old City and the Mount of Olives before me I could not resist! So I ventured to the Old City, an easy journey since Notre Dame, my home while in Jerusalem, is just across the street from the New Gate of the Old City. I went immediately to the Church of the Holy Sepulchre and there were very few people there. So I went into the tomb of Jesus without having to wait. I could not find words for prayer. I had to assume that God could read the joy and awe I felt at being able to return to this most holy of places in this most complex of cities. I did stop at the shrine venerated as Mary's place at the foot of Calvary and said a special prayer for all who mourn and whose hearts are troubled.

As I left the Church I carried with me the final verses of Psalm 122: *For the peace of Jerusalem pray: "May those who love you prosper! May peace be within your ramparts, prosperity within your towers." For family and friends I say, "May peace be yours." For the house of the Lord, our God, I pray, "May blessings be yours."*

Walk About Zion, Go Round About Her, Number Her Towers

Where to begin on this first full day of visiting in Jerusalem? I decided to take my cue from the Psalmist: *Go about Zion, walk all around it, note the number of its towers. Consider the ramparts, examine its citadels, that you may tell future generations; "Yes, so might is God, our God who leads us always!" (Psalm 48:12-14)*

What I thought would be a two hour walk around the walls of the Old City turned into a six hour adventure and I only saw five of the seven gates that are still open as entrances to the city! One of the blessings of a lengthy time here is that I do not have to rush in order to see things. If something at a turn of the corner raises my curiosity, I am free to explore. Or as happened this morning when I rounded the old city wall at the Zion Gate, my eye caught sight of the Mount of Olives. I had to sit for a time and allow myself to be spellbound by the beauty of the mountain against a sky too blue for words. How could I pass up the opportunity to sit and watch the young children in the Jewish Quarter running from school, happy to be free for another afternoon? It is on days like this that I recognize what a gift, what a grace, leisure time can be.

The walls of the Old City of Jerusalem date to 1537 when Suleiman the Magnificent ordered them to be rebuilt after they had been dismantled in 1219. For the most part, Suleiman's walls follow the line of those they replaced, but for some reason no one seems to know, his builders did not include Mount Zion (David's City) in their plans. So today David's City is outside the walls, but still it is recognized as the original site where the city began around 1000 B.C. when the young King made what was a Jebusite stronghold his capital. The story is told in the second book of Samuel, beginning with chapter five.

I have long been fascinated by the Gates of the Old City. Their numbers and names have varied throughout the long history of Jerusalem. Studying the history, geography and archeology of Jerusalem is like trying to put together a three-dimensional puzzle. The same is true in reading the history of the ancient city walls and city gates. For example, in the southeast corner of the city wall three ancient gates, now walled in, are visible. One of these gates may have been the gate through which Jesus entered the city for his trial. But since it is not certain where Pontius Pilate was staying when he came to keep order during the feast of Passover, it is not certain what gate would have been used by the guards who brought Jesus to Pilate that Good Friday morning after he was questioned by the high priest Caiaphas the night before.

Even though we will never be certain about the exact location of the biblical events that are a part of our spiritual history, trying to fit the pieces together has the power to enhance our appreciation of the richness of our life of faith. I think that is one of the reasons I treasure the opportunity to come to the Holy Land.

This morning, as I sat looking at the Mount of Olives, the Kidron Valley, the Valley of Gehenna and the Temple Mount for a long time, I was able to piece together the geography and history of places that play an important role in the heritage of our faith. But even after connecting the dots, I was left with a feeling of awe before the *MYSTERY* of it all. With every step I take, beneath every rock I overturn, behind all of the historical data, the geographical details and archeological findings I read about, there is a God who entered my human history in the person of His only begotten Son Jesus, that through Him I might share in the salvation He has promised to his beloved in every age.

The purpose of a pilgrimage to the Holy Land it not to visit a place; it is to find a God: the God made visible in His Son Jesus, who walked these lands; and with each step made not only this place, but the whole world holy.

Just Let Go

I have always marveled at the way Jesus was able to look at the world around him and draw spiritual insights from even the simplest of things: the lilies of the field, a mustard seed, a barren fig tree. Perhaps that is what made him a great teacher. He began with what was ordinary and familiar, and then led people to a profound spiritual truth. His methodology invites us to look at the experiences that are a part of our lives and consider if they might have more to say to us than what first appears.

I think of this in light of an experience yesterday at the Tower of David – the Museum of the City of Jerusalem. The ancient chambers of the Citadel have been converted into exhibition halls outlining each major period in Jerusalem's long history. A series of walkways within the inner courtyard connect the exhibition rooms. The tour begins with a breathtaking view of the Old City and Mount of Olives from the top of one of the towers.

I have a fear of heights that manifests itself at the strangest times. I can fly in an airplane or go to the top of the Empire State Building with no problem. But asking me to climb a ladder to change a light bulb is like asking me to scale Mount Everest blind-folded, unescorted and on crutches! So when I climbed to the top of the tower to take in the view I was happy to see the enclosed stone stairways; those I can handle. So I concluded that I would have no problem along the way. Wrong! When I left one exhibition hall to continue the tour I discovered I was on top of an open metal stairway hanging on the side of one of the tower walls. "Panic" is not too strong a word in this situation!

I had a decision to make and there were several options. I could turn around and exit the museum the way I had entered. God bless those enclosed stone stairways! But I had just started the tour and leaving meant not finishing what was, up to this point, a wonderful experience. I could go down the stairway on my bottom. Don't laugh! I did just that many years ago when I found myself in a similar situation on an open wooden staircase on the side of a cliff 400 meters above the Dead Sea at Masada. No one told me that after the cable car ride up the mountain there was a staircase! The problem here was one of pride. Since I don't speak Hebrew or Arabic I am already convinced that everyone in Jerusalem is always talking about me. Now all I needed was to give them more ammunition by climbing down a staircase one cheek at a time! The final option was to bite the bullet and go down the stairs like most people with my pride and dignity in check. I decided that if I stretched out my arms, held onto both handrails, and looked straight ahead, I might be able to pull this off. I estimated there were about 40 steps and if I counted each step I would be encouraged along the way as I made progress.

All went well until I hit step number ten. That is when one of the museum workers decided to come up the steps as I was coming down! Now what? Go back up and start all over again? No way. I was not about to undo eight weeks of sabbatical by inviting that much stress back into my life! I could start screaming at the attendant to go back. But at just that moment I forgot the Hebrew word for "retreat." Come to think of it, I do not think it is in their vocabulary! There was only one choice. I was going to have to let go of one of the rails and let the man pass. So I dug down deep inside looking for that gift of courage that was given to me at confirmation, and when the man was two steps away I let go of the left rail and let him pass. Mind you, I did not tempt the Holy Spirit. As soon as he passed I held on again for dear life and started: eleven, twelve, thirteen…

As I think back on the experience, maybe going down on my bottom would not have been so bad. I probably looked like Lucy in that episode of "I Love Lucy" when she comes down the staircase in the Carmen Miranda headdress!

Also looking back, there are times when living means letting go of our fears. Not letting go means leaving the museum of life not having experienced all there is to experience. Or not letting go might mean going through life on our backside rather that with our heads held high like the children of God that we are. I do not have to go about life looking for open metal staircases to climb to prove that I can do it. But when they show up in the path of my living I have to decide if I am going to let an irrational fear keep me from experiencing life fully; or, if I am going to be willing to let go of at least one hand, trusting that for a few moments I can meet the challenge before me. Maybe that is why we like to sing: "Be not afraid, I go before you always…"

Today I learned that it is possible to walk from the Jaffa Gate to the Dung Gate on top of the ramparts of the Old City Wall. Don't even think about it!!! Shalom.

Mount Zion On Confirmation Day

This morning I went to Mount Zion to pray at the Cenacle for the students from my parish of Saint Joseph who will be receiving the Sacrament of Confirmation today. The Cenacle, or Upper Room, is venerated as the site where Jesus celebrated the Last Supper with his disciples. It is also the same upper room we read about in the Acts of the Apostles where the apostles, Mary, the disciples and the holy women gathered for prayer after the Ascension of Jesus. It is in that upper room, on the feast of Pentecost, that they received the Holy Spirit as Jesus had promised. Since I could not be present with our Confirmands I thought this might be the best gift that I could offer them on this most significant day in their faith journey. I prayed for them, for Bishop Kevin Rhoades, for their families and for their sponsors.

Mount Zion, site of the ancient city of King David, is easily reached through the Zion Gate in the wall of the Old City. In Arabic it is called "Bab al-Nabi Da'ud" or the "Gate of the Prophet David" since it is believed that the Tomb of King David is located on Mount Zion.

The Gate is located where the Armenian Quarter meets the Jewish Quarter in the Old City. Each of the city gates has its own unique character. I am not sure why, but the Zion Gate is my favorite. Like the other more ancient gates of the city, it is "L-shaped." That design may have worked well for camels and donkeys, but how cars and trucks in the present day are able to maneuver through the "L" is a wonder to behold!

The Zion Gate played an important role in the Jewish War of Independence in 1948 when the Jews were forced from this portion of the city and the Jewish Quarter (including the Western Wall) became a part of Jordan. In the Six Day War of 1967 the Jews occupied the Old City and the Jewish Quarter was rebuilt. The stones surrounding the Gate give evidence of gun and mortar fire.

In the Holy Land it is not certain that those venerated as holy sites are the actual locations where biblical events took place. The present building housing the Upper Room dates to a reconstruction of an earlier building by the Franciscans in 1335. It was on or near this place that the Crusader Church of Saint Mary of Zion was located. The earliest record associating this site with the Last Supper and Pentecost is from the 5th century.

The Franciscans were expelled from this site by Suleiman the Magnificent on March 18, 1523. Since the Upper Room is located over the site venerated as the Tomb of David, and since the Moslems regard David as a prophet, Suleiman decreed: "It is neither just nor appropriate that this most noble place remain in the hands of the infidels and that, in obedience to their impious customs, their feet foul the places sanctified by the prophets who have a right to our complete veneration." The Moslems did expel the Franciscans from the site but it was regained by the Jews in 1967. The complex now houses a Yeshiva, and the Tomb of David is a synagogue and a National Monument of the State of Israel. Many devout Jews come here to pray at the tomb of King David on Mount Zion, the city of David.

This means that since the Upper Room is no longer used as a mosque, it is open to all visitors. Pilgrims do pray in the Upper Room but it is not used as a place to celebrate Mass. The exception was when Pope John Paul II came to the Holy Land in the Jubilee Year 2000 and was given permission to celebrate Mass there with twelve bishops concelebrating. After the Mass he asked to be left alone in the Upper Room and there he prayed in solitude for thirty minutes.

In some ways it is disappointing to see the Upper Room so bare, since this place is so significant in our sacramental history. Here we commemorate the institution of the Eucharist, Confirmation and Holy Orders. In our Catholic Christian tradition we rely on signs and symbols to express the mysteries of our faith, and yet the Upper Room is without decoration. However, if you read the right guidebook and know where to look there is one hopeful sign. Scripture Scholar Father Stephen Doyle tells his pilgrim readers to look at the capitol of one of the pillars in the upper room. There you will find a carving of a pelican piercing her breast in order to feed her young, a symbol of the way we in our Catholic tradition, are fed by our sacramental life.

When I entered the Upper Room it was filled with pilgrims, many singing and praying together. I waited for a time and eventually they left and I had the Upper Room to myself for about five minutes! I had a feeling of what it must have been like for Pope John Paul to be alone in this very special place. I was able to find the carving of the pelican and my sacramental sensibilities were satisfied. I left feeling a kinship with our Confirmands on their special day and with all who treasure our sacramental life as Catholic Christians.

Shopping In The Old City

It is difficult to describe the Old City of Jerusalem. Think of the street scenes at the Cairo Bazaar in "Raiders of the Lost Ark" and you get the picture. When it comes to wandering in the Old City I learned the other day that I am no Indiana Jones!

To say that the merchants are aggressive does not quite capture it; because even when you are not shopping, they are selling. From my previous visits to Jerusalem I learned a few things. When asked, to be polite I used to always say that whatever the seller was showing me was nice. Rule number one: Do not say that anything in a shop is nice. To a merchant that means you want to buy it. And even if you have no use for a three-foot copper Turkish coffee server from the Ayyubid period, since you said it was nice, the seller is sure you want to take it home.

Rule number two: when walking through the Old City pretend that the only languages you speak are those of Middle Earth from *The Lord of the Rings*. They might be the only languages the merchants have not mastered, at least with enough proficiency to draw you in "to show you my shop." Because the minute you respond to a merchant calling out to you in English, you are trapped.

Rule number three: there are no Arabic words for "just browsing." The concept does not exist in the Suq. If you looked at it, and heaven forbid you picked it up, you might as well assume that you will be finding a way to pack it in your suitcase!

Rule number four: I have observed that the African pilgrims love to shop and they seem to buy a lot of luggage. It is amazing to me that shops specializing in jewelry or sandals suddenly have a tower of Samsonite look-alikes on the front steps the minute the Africans arrive. So the quickest way of getting through the market to your destination is to place yourself in the midst of an African pilgrimage.

The merchants will quickly lose all interest in you as they demonstrate the size and strength of the steamer trunk that every African must have to return home a happy pilgrim!

The other day I was making my way back to the hotel after a visit to the Church of the Holy Sepulchre and a falafel and diet coke lunch. When I reached the David Street Suq I took a deep breath, put my head down, went into my Elvish trance, waited for the next group of unsuspecting African tourists who would be running defense for me, and set out for the Jaffa Gate. I do not know how it happened but in a few moments I found myself face-to-face with a young enterprising merchant who said: "You have been promising me for days to come into my shop. Today is the day!" I told him I was not shopping and he said he only wanted to show me his shop. "No need to buy anything, my friend." Well, what else have I got to do today?

Before I knew what had happened he produced a chair from nowhere, seated me in the center of his shop, handed me a glass of mint tea and explained to me that he was a Palestinian and that business was very bad. I said "I understand." Big mistake. Addendum. Rule number five: Never say you understand ANYTHING.

With that he asked me my favorite color. What is the Elvish word for purple? I forgot for the moment so I said "purple." And then, with the flair of Merlin, he produced the most beautiful Persian rug with subtle shades of purple, green and red and placed it in my lap. The purple number was followed by something he called the "family rug." It also was beautiful and joined the purple beauty on my lap. Next came a deep blue oval carpet with deer running around the edges. "You don't like the fringes, I cut them off. No harm to the carpet." I could have sworn he told me it was a 300,000 thread count. The unraveling of rugs continued and in a matter of minutes I was looking like Marco Polo returning to Venice after a successful visit to the East.

Now, if the truth be told, I had thought about looking at carpets when I got to Kusadasi in Turkey. How did he know? But why wait until Turkey? I mean, each carpet here was more beautiful than the next. And single-handedly I would be changing the Palestinian economy. So there I was, draped in Persian silk, my eyes sparkling like Tiffany's with each new rug placed on my lap. And then I did it. I almost sealed my fate then and there when I spoke the words every merchant in the Suq longs to hear from an American: "How much?" Rule number six: Never ask how much.

Boy, this guy was good. Without saying a word or missing a beat, he cleared my lap and selected two rugs. He folded them into suitcase size and placed them in my hands with these words: "You are a man with good taste. I can tell that these are the two you like the best." How did he know? Damn those Tiffany eyes! "Since you are my friend and my first customer today, for you, five-thousand dollars for both of them." Five thousand dollars? Please God, do not let me spill mint tea on one of these rugs or I will be emptying my IRA account when I get home! I knew that five thousand dollars was the beginning bargaining number, but even so. Five thousand dollars? I began to think less in terms of "Persian carpet" and more in terms of "Persian coaster."

Now how do I get out of this mess? Well, with a sigh of regret I simply handed the rugs back and reminded him that I was not shopping today and had no intention of buying a carpet. I will take that lie up with my confessor when I get home. I knew what was coming next. "Well then, tell me" he said, "What price would change your mind." I explained again that I could not name a price because I did not want a carpet. He then slipped one of the carpets back into my hands (the purple one) and said: "How much will you give me for your favorite?" I handed the carpet back and said I was not interested. He was beginning to get the picture but was not giving up just yet. "I want you to take both carpets back to your hotel and think about it. I trust you my friend." Again I explained that I was not interested. He gave in, with a deep sigh, and made me promise that I would continue to think about it while I was in Jerusalem.

Then he really struck a low blow. "You see that shop across the street? That is mine too. That is where I sell cheap souvenirs to tourists.

Perhaps you would like to buy something there for your wife?" So much for my good taste! I explained that I had no wife. Why was I letting this happen? Go back to your Middle Earth Elvish mode and get out of here. "Then for your girlfriend," he continued. I told him I had no girlfriend. Afraid of what he might suggest next I took his card and went looking for a bigger group of African pilgrims to get me to the Jaffa Gate.

A Windy Morning On The Mount Of Olives Surrounded By The Lord's Prayer

The Mount of Olives. The very name brings to mind gospel events that are a part of our spiritual history and stories that continue to inspire us no matter how often we hear them. For those who have been blessed to go to Jerusalem on pilgrimage, hearing "The Mount of Olives" brings to mind never forgotten images of the Mosque of the Ascension, the Church of the Pater Noster, the Chapel of Dominus Flavit and the Garden of Gethsemane.

Long before I arrived here I have been praying for the peace of Jerusalem. Now that I am here I have added the installation of escalators to my intentions! Since that has not happened yet this morning I took a taxi to the top of the Mount of Olives and wandered down the winding road that leads to the Garden of Gethsemane. Atop the mountain is a view of Mount Zion (the ancient city of David), Mount Moriah (the Temple Mount), the Kidron, Hinnon and Tyropoeon Valleys and the Garden of Gethsemane that one can never forget.

Just in front of the Seven Arches Hotel there is an observation platform that is often used by newscasters when reporting on events in Jerusalem, where it is easy to see why. All of the ancient city and surrounding areas are present before you, and the villages of Bethpage, Bethany and the Judean desert are just over the hill behind you. I was happy to see that the same camel and donkey drivers were present from my previous visits! "You want picture? Just five shekels!"

Describing all of the special places on the Mount of Olives in one entry would be too much. For today, I decided to concentrate on the Church of the Pater Noster and share some thoughts about the other places in the days ahead.

Today's Church of the Pater Noster (Our Father) and the adjoining Carmelite Monastery date to the late 1800's and were built over the sight of the Crusader Chapel of 1160, which was destroyed in 1345. The history of this place goes back to the fourth century when the Emperor Constantine, at the urging of his mother Helena, built three churches over significant mystical caves in the Holy Land: the cave of the Nativity in Bethlehem, the cave of Calvary, and the cave on the Mount of Olives associated with the Ascension of Jesus and the place where he taught his disciples in private. Constantine's Mount of Olives Church was called the Eleona, the Church of the Olive Groves.

At the end of the fourth century the site for commemorating the Ascension was moved a short distance up the mountain to the present site of the Mosque of the Ascension. The Eleona was then associated exclusively with the place where Jesus taught his disciples about the conflict between good and evil (Matthew 24 and 25).

According to a brochure published at the site, the cave or grotto was where Jesus and his disciples gathered in secret away from the watchful eyes of the Roman guard. It was here that Nicodemus met secretly with Jesus, an event recorded (without mention of place) in the third chapter of John's gospel. In the late fourth century a pilgrim named Egeria kept a detailed diary of her visit to the Holy Land which survives today. She reported that on Tuesday of Holy Week these chapters from Matthew's gospel were read in the cave of the Eleona. And on Holy Thursday evening, "sitting where Jesus himself sat," the Bishop of Jerusalem would read the Lord's Last Supper Discourse from the Gospel of John, chapters 15-17.

Constantine's church was set on fire by the Persians in 614 and completely destroyed by the Moslems in 638. The grotto beneath and the Eleona Church were covered over and their ruins were not rediscovered until 1870. In 1910 the grotto was excavated and today is preserved underneath the ruins of the Constantinian church.

After the destruction of the Church in the sixth century, the significance of the place shifted and the site was remembered exclusively as the place where Jesus taught his disciples the Lord's Prayer, the Pater Noster. That was the ongoing tradition when the Crusaders built their chapel here in the 12th century. At that time pilgrims reported seeing marble plaques with the Our Father inscribed in Hebrew, Greek and Latin. That tradition continues today with ceramic plaques of the Our Father lining the walls of the courtyard and monastery cloister in over 60 languages, including a Braille plaque in Hebrew and English.

I had the good fortune today to meet the prioress of the Carmelite monastery, a nun from Madagascar, who cares for this holy place. I carried greetings to her from the Carmelite nuns in Elysburg, Pennsylvania where I served as chaplain during my years as a campus minister in Bloomsburg University. She was most gracious and, in turn, wanted to be remembered to the Elysburg Carmel. When the group of pilgrims from Mechanicsburg comes to Jerusalem at the end of March, we will be having Mass at this wonderful place of prayer.

Often the sacred sites in the Holy Land are busy with guides talking and pilgrims taking pictures so it is a challenging to find a quiet place for meditation. Ironically, the most difficult place to pray in Jerusalem is the Church of the Holy Sepulchre, the place of Jesus' resurrection! The Pater Noster site is an exception. There is something about the enclosure on the side of the Mount of Olives that provides a calm setting encouraging prayer. What better way to pray than to use the words that Jesus gave to those closest to him.

I personally like the account of the story that comes to us from the Gospel of Luke, chapter eleven. In Luke's version the disciples asked Jesus to teach them to pray as John had taught his disciples. Jesus did not initiate the teaching. Rather, like all good teachers, he waited until they were ready to receive what he would offer. They came to him when their hearts were ready. Only then did he teach. The same is true for us.

The best lessons about prayer are learned from the ways we communicate with one another every day. Did you ever say to someone who asks you a question: "Give me a minute. Let me finish what I am doing and I will give you my undivided attention." Or have you ever said to someone else: "Stop what you are doing! I need you to listen to me now!" That is what happened when the disciples came to Jesus. They had put down what they were doing long enough to pay attention to his lesson on prayer. They had arrived at a place in their relationship with Jesus where they trusted that whatever he would say would be more important than what they themselves were thinking.

It challenges me to ask myself before praying: "Am I coming to the Lord with all the answers already worked out in my head?" If so, then my prayer becomes a dueling match with the Lord as I try to get him to see things from the wisdom of my vantage point! Or am I willing to come to Jesus in prayer because I trust HIS wisdom, HIS light, HIS grace? I think that is what it means when we say *thy kingdom come, thy will be done.*

I am also struck by the timing of the disciples' request. At the end of chapter ten, just before teaching the Our Father, Jesus is in the home of Martha and Mary in Bethany, just over the hill from the Church of the Pater Noster. In that story Jesus tells Martha that there are times when she is to sit at the feet of the Master, as her sister Mary was doing. *"Martha, Martha, you are anxious and worried about many things. There is need of only one thing. Mary has chosen the better part and it will not be taken from her."* (Luke 10:38-42)

In the very next verse, the beginning of chapter eleven, Jesus practiced what he had been preaching. He went out to a certain place (the grotto nearby?) to pray, to sit at the feet of his heavenly Father. It was when the disciples saw Jesus praying that they made their request: "Lord, teach us to pray."

I ended my wanderings on the Mount of Olives today in Gethsemane at the Church of All Nations. It is the place where Jesus went to pray after the Last Supper, the event we call the Agony in the Garden. I will share more about that most beautiful church at another time. As I entered, a pilgrim group had just finished Mass and another was waiting to enter the area around the rock of Gethsemane to pray. In a quiet corner, near the entrance of the church, stood an older woman gently singing "alleluia" over and over again. If you had rushed by her you probably would not have heard her song. I chose to sit near the back of the church to avoid the noise of the crowd. It was then that I heard her singing in a rhythm that sounded almost like a lullaby. Her quiet chant called me to a prayerful mood and let me forget about the activity and camera flashes all around the intentionally darkened church.

The experience made me think of the prophetess Anna, the daughter of Phanuel of the tribe of Asher, who used to come to the temple praying day and night (Luke 2:36-38). She was there when Joseph and Mary brought the Child Jesus to the temple at the time of their purification, according to the law of the Moses.

I was not the only one who was moved by her prayer. Soon after I arrived the church was closing for lunch! As I left I saw another pilgrim thanking the woman for her gentle prayers. Her quiet song moved me to say "Lord, teach me to pray as John taught his disciples."

Why Was Jesus Weeping?

Midway down the western slope of the Mount of Olives, along a windy road where Palm Sunday Pilgrims re-enact Jesus' entry into Jerusalem, there is a small chapel called "Dominus Flavit" (Jesus wept). The site commemorates the story told in the Gospel of Luke, chapter nineteen.

Jesus began his entry into the holy city from Bethpage and Bethany on the eastern slope of the mountain. We are told that the multitude of disciples began to rejoice in a loud voice saying: *"Blessed is the King who comes in the name of the Lord! Peace in heaven and glory in the highest!"* And then Luke continues: *"As he drew near, he saw the city and wept over it, saying, 'If this day you only knew what makes for peace - but now it is hidden from your eyes. For the days are coming upon you when your enemies will raise a palisade against you; they will encircle you and hem you in on all sides. They will smash you to the ground and your children within you, and they will not leave one stone upon another within you because you did not recognize the time of your visitation.'"* (Luke 19: 41-44)

Were more ominous words ever spoken by Jesus; words that have such a different tenor from anything else he said during his ministry? There seems to be no turning back, no reason for hope. The die has been cast; Jerusalem will be destroyed and her inhabitants killed. It is no wonder Jesus wept.

I must admit that when I read this passage yesterday while visiting Dominus Flavit, it left me quite unsettled. Oh yes, I had read it many times before. But reading it here in a chapel overlooking the Old City and the Temple Mount, places marked for centuries by violence and bloodshed, caused me to sit up and take notice of the stark reality of Jesus' words.

Like the Church of the Pater Noster near the top of the Mount of Olives, this holy site lends itself to easy mediation. I was fortunate Cyprus a group of pilgrims had just left and I was alone in the place. The setting is picture perfect. The chapel is nestled among a grove of Cyprus trees and spring flowers were in bloom. The gate attendant pointed to poppies blooming nearby and wanted to know if we had them in America. "Yes," I answered, "but not for three more months!"

The chapel was designed by Antonio Barluzzi, the 20th century architect responsible for many of the important churches in the Holy Land. His works include the chapel in the Shepherd's Field in Bethlehem, the Church of All Nations in the Garden of Gethsemane just down the hill from Dominus Flavit, and the Church of the Transfiguration on Mount Tabor to name a few. The great travel writer H.V. Morton observes that in his designs Barluzzi tries to "express an emotional response to the Gospel story." He designed Dominus Flavit to look like a tear drop. The church and its serene setting are indeed a place where tears are easily shed; first by Jesus and then by all who are sensitive to the tensions and tragedies that are a part of the fiber of this most holy and yet most complex of cities. Hermann Melville said of the city: *"The air over Jerusalem is saturated with prayers and dreams... it's hard to breathe."*

Today I was again made aware of the tensions of the city when I went to lunch. I had spent the morning reading and decided to go for a walk and visit a small Thai restaurant in the new city not far from the hotel. I placed my order and waited. It is amazing what you can communicate with only two words of Hebrew: shalom and toda (thank you)! I took a seat at a small table next to three young Israeli soldiers, two women and one man. Only when they got up to get their order did I see their semi-automatic rifles leaning next to their chairs.

If this day you only knew what make for peace – but now it is hidden from your eyes.

Praying At The Western Wall

Perhaps no other sight in Jerusalem is as recognizable as the Western Wall. And with good reason. It's historical, religious, social and political significance cannot be overstated because, for centuries, the Wall is where Jews have gone to pray to lament the loss of the temple. It is sometime called the Wailing Wall. It is more than that: it is an open air synagogue where Sabbath services and Bar Mitzvah ceremonies are held, and where anyone who enters respectfully is invited to pray. A tradition of placing small slips of paper with prayer intentions into the crevices of wall has earned it the name "God's mailbox." One of the most historic and touching images of this holy site was John Paul II placing a prayer for peace in the wall during his visit in March of the Jubilee Year 2000. It was above this sight that the Holy of Holies of the temple was located so the place is associated with the presence of God. It is said that Menachem Begin told Jimmy Carter that talking to God in Jerusalem is only a local call!

The Western Wall is actually a retaining wall from the First and Second Temples. The first temple was built by King Solomon around the year 950 B.C. on Mount Moriah (I Kings 5-6). Mount Moriah was a threshing floor next to Mount Zion that King David purchased from Araunah the Jebusite for fifty shekels of silver (2 Samuel 24:18-25). The temple was built to house the Ark of the Covenant. Solomon's temple was destroyed by the Babylonians in 587 B.C. Fifty years later, when the Jews returned from captivity in Babylon, the temple was rebuilt with the help of King Cyrus of Persia. After desecration by the Hellenists in the second century B.C., the Temple was rededicated by the priestly family of the Maccabees, an event recalled each year at the celebration of Hanukkah. The second temple was rebuilt and enlarged by Herod the Great just before the time of Jesus. That temple was destroyed, along with all of Jerusalem, in 70 A.D. by the Romans under the command of Titus. The Arch of Titus in the Roman Forum has a marble relief depicting articles being carried from the temple during the siege of Jerusalem.

The Jews had intermittent access to the Western Wall and Temple Mount during the centuries following the destruction of the city. But in 691 A.D., with the building of Jerusalem's first great mosque, the Dome of the Rock, the Moslems denied access to the Temple Mount to non-believers. The Holy of Holies, the sacred part of the temple housing the Ark of the Covenant, was built over the rock where Abram was to sacrifice Isaac. In turn, the Dome of the Rock was built over the sight of the Holy of Holies because it was believed that it was from there the prophet Mohammed ascended into heaven. The most dramatic event in recent times occurred in 1967 during the Six Day War when the Israelis took possession of the entire Old City from the Jordanians, who had control of the area since the War of 1948 after the establishment of the State of Israel. Since that time the importance of the site has grown in stature and the Western Wall is a sign of the sovereignty of the State of Israel. New recruits into the Israeli army are often sworn in at the Wall.

I remember visiting the Wall during my first visit to Jerusalem in December of 1975 but I do not remember anything about the experience of praying there. When I came in March of 2000 I prayed at the Wall but found the time to be unsettling. Although all are invited to pray there, I had a sense that somehow I was trespassing at a place where I did not belong. The experience in 2005 was different. Perhaps the site of John Paul II praying at the Wall provided me with a different perspective. This week on a sunny afternoon I was able to pray at the Western Wall for all of the people of the Middle East who hold this place sacred, but for whom peace is so elusive. I also prayed for renewed understanding among all people of good will and for all of my Jewish friends who celebrate the holiness of this place.

Transfiguration

Each year, on the Second Sunday of Lent, we read the account of the Transfiguration, surely one of the most dramatic events in the life of Jesus. This liturgical year we hear the story from the ninth chapter of Luke's gospel. As is always the case, each of the gospel stories can stand on its own; but when we see an individual story in the context of the rest of the gospel, its meaning is enhanced.

The Transfiguration is no exception. We appreciate it as a glimpse of the glory that will come to Jesus after his resurrection. We also appreciate it as a promise of the glory that will be ours at the end of our lives when we see Christ face-to-face. But we ought to continue reading after the Transfiguration story ends in order to get the "rest of the story." We learn that, on next day, after they had come down from the mountain, the ministry of Jesus continued when a man brought his son to him. "Teacher, *I beg you, look upon my son; he is my only child,*" said the man. "*A spirit seizes him, and he suddenly screams and it convulses him until he foams at the mouth; it releases him only with difficulty, wearing him out,*" the desperate man continues. The story goes on but in the end Jesus rebukes the unclean spirit, heals the boy and gives him back to his father. (Luke 9"37-43)

There is no more perfect visual rendering of the Transfiguration than the one painted by Raphael in the 16th century. Today it is found in the Art Gallery of the Vatican Museum. A mosaic of the painting is in Saint Peter's Basilica. It depicts the Transfiguration but the lower section of the painting also shows the healing that took place on the next day. It is that story that completes the Transfiguration event.

Peter, James and John knew the privilege of the Transfiguration moment. In fact, Peter tells Jesus: "*Master, it is good that we are here; let us make three tents, one for you, one for Moses, and one for Elijah.*"

But the vision ends with a cloud overshadowing them and the disciples becoming frightened as they hear a voice from the cloud proclaim: "This is my chosen Son; listen to him." And after the voice had spoken Jesus was alone, and they fell silent and came down from the mountain to meet the man seeking a favor from Jesus for his son.

The glory of heaven was to be Jesus' on another day. Now his ministry of preaching the kingdom of God and healing those who would be a part of that kingdom would continue until the day of his death. On the mountain Peter misunderstood the whole of Jesus' mission. It was not a mission of glory but a mission of service that would lead to his glory.

The lesson taught to Peter, James and John has much to say to us today when we gather for Mass and hear the Transfiguration Gospel. When we come to Mass we appreciate a time away from the routine and challenge of our daily living. Liturgy is a foretaste of the heavenly banquet and so we are right to expect that our prayer together will offer us a measure of rest and a promise of peace. But the word "liturgy" comes from the Greek word for "work." Liturgy is work not only for the priest who celebrates, but also for the musicians who lead us in song, the readers who proclaim the scriptures and those who serve in other liturgical ministries. It is also work for those who attend: the work of active participation, the work of attentive listening, and the work of being a supportive, prayerful presence to those who share the experience with us.

Peter, James and John missed the "work" of the Transfiguration moment; they fell asleep! Perhaps that is why they misunderstood its meaning and were silent as they left the mountain. We are challenged to do the work of liturgy so that when we leave Mass, when we come down from the mountain, we are prepared to do the work of Christian living – the work that brings about justice, promotes peace, and offers forgiveness.

There is a danger in seeing the Mass as an escape from what is difficult in our living. We do not escape when we come to Mass;

rather, we stand apart for a time so that we can gain a better perspective of what our life means in light of the gospel call to discipleship. With that new perspective, hopefully given in a scripture-based homily and strengthened in the Eucharist, we are better prepared to leave the mountain and go about our day-to-day gospel living once again.

A Visit To Bethany – Encountering The Wall

When Jesus traveled to Jerusalem from the Galilee he stayed in Bethany at the house of Lazarus and his two sisters, Martha and Mary. Some of the best known and most loved gospel stories take place there: the story of Mary reclining at the feet of Jesus while Martha is taking care of the details of hospitality (Luke 10:38-42); the anointing of Jesus by the unnamed woman just before his death at the house of Simon the Leper (Matthew 26:6-13); and certainly one of the most dramatic of stories, the raising of Lazarus from the dead as told in the eleventh chapter of the Gospel of John.

Today I traveled to Bethany to visit this place that played such a significant role in the life and ministry of Jesus. Bethany is called "El-Azariyeh" in Arabic. It is named after Lazarus because Moslems also acknowledge his being raised from the dead. The village is located along the road to Jericho on the eastern slope of the Mount of Olives, just three kilometers from Jerusalem; but today it might as well have been 50 kilometers. These days a cab going from Jerusalem to Jericho must go around the Mount of Olives and enter the town from the opposite side. This is because Bethany is separated from Jerusalem by "the wall," the protective barrier built by the Israeli government separating the Palestine territory from the state of Israel.

"I could have had you there in ten minutes," the Arab cabdriver told us. "And it would have cost you 50 shekels. Now it takes longer and costs you double." The sight of the wall and the checkpoint is startling, as is the contrast between the city of Jerusalem and the village of Bethany just over the Mount of Olives. Most guidebooks consider Bethany a part of Jerusalem, but the two could not be more different. When we arrived in the town a large group of Arabs had gathered along the side of the road. We asked our driver what they were doing. "Waiting for the U.N. workers who will bring them food and aid," he said. "In Palestine, we wait all the time."

One of the hotel restaurant workers named Johnny, a Christian who lives in Bethlehem, told me the same thing. It should take him only thirty minutes to get to work each day, but when he has to be there at 6:30 a.m. he gets up at 3:00 because he never knows how long it will take to get through the wall at the checkpoint just outside of Bethlehem. When we go through airport security and there is a problem with someone, they are taken aside and the problem is dealt with while the line continues. Not so at the wall. When there is a question or concern, the line stops and everyone waits until the problem is settled. A young, energetic man like Johnny, who works hard to provide for his wife and child, never knows from one day to the next whether he will be able to get to work at all, let alone on time.

For some time I have been reading about the Israeli-Palestinian situation from every angle (political, social and religious) and from every point of view (pro-Palestinian and pro-Israeli) and I can tell you, being here does not help to clarify the issues at all. If anything, their complexity becomes even more apparent with each new person I meet and each new story I hear. When I talk with Christian-Arab Johnny I wonder why the Israeli government cannot see the folly of the wall. And when I hear about a Jewish father who will not take his family out to dinner for fear that a suicide bomber from the West Bank might make his way through the restaurant door, I understand why the wall seems to offer an added measure of security for the protection of the state of Israel.

The 1954 Franciscan Church of Saint Lazarus in Bethany is bright, airy and filled with mosaics that tell the story of the friendship that Jesus had with Lazarus and Martha and Mary; a friendship that offered calm in the midst of chaos and hope in the midst of sorrow. The entrance to the tomb of Lazarus just up the street leads to a narrow, steep stairway descending twenty-five feet into the earth below. Though the tomb is empty it is a place of darkness, sorrow and loss. These days it seems that this holy land lives somewhere between these two worlds. Just when a hand of friendship is extended and peace seems to be on the horizon, another storm cloud appears. Old hatreds and new fears emerge and all sides descend into a tomb of suspicion and despair. There does not seem to be anyone who is able to speak to both sides a commanding "Come out of your fears and untie the hatreds that bind your hearts and minds." So not only the Palestinians but the whole world waits for a time and a place when the words of Isaiah come to pass: *There shall always be rejoicing and happiness in what I create; for I create Jerusalem and exult in my people. No longer shall the sound of weeping be heard there, or the sound of crying. (Isaiah 65:18-19)*

The Third Sunday Of Lent At The Church Of The Holy Sepulchre

Wherever to begin? Perhaps with a few words about the Church of the Holy Sepulchre.

The Basilica of the Holy Sepulchre incorporates both the Mount of the Crucifixion and the Tomb of Jesus. In the fourth century the Empress Helena, the mother of Emperor Constantine, found what she believed to be the true cross of Jesus in a cistern near the site of the rock of Calvary. The location was the site of long abandoned quarries and ancient tombs. This place of her discovery is also under the roof of the present Church, two levels beneath the main floor.

At the time of Helena and Constantine the area was home to the Forum of the Roman Emperor Hadrian, who, in 132 A.D., rebuilt Jerusalem as the capital of the province of Syria Palestina. He filled in the quarries and erected two temples on the site, one to Jupiter Capitolina, the god of Rome, and one to Aprodite. These temples were razed by Constantine when the tomb of Jesus was discovered in 326 A.D. and the building of the Basilica began. The "Martyrium of Golgotha" was dedicated in 335 A.D., but the remainder of the church incorporating the Tomb of Jesus was not completed until sometime after the year 340 A.D.

The Basilica of Constantine was destroyed by the Persians in 614 A.D. and was rebuilt soon after by the Patriarch Modestus. His church, following the same lines as the Constantinian Basilica, was destroyed by the Caliph Hakim in 1009. The Church was rebuilt and was open to the Crusaders who arrive there in 1099 A.D., but for financial reasons it was considerably smaller than the original church of Helena and Constantine. With some modifications made by the Crusaders and repairs following fires and earthquakes throughout the centuries, the eleventh century Church of the Holy Sepulchre is what pilgrims see today.

If all of this sounds confusing, it is nothing compared to the complex arrangement that governs the jurisdiction of the Basilica today. The Church is divided among Latin Catholics, Greek Orthodox, Armenians, Syrians and Copts. Although the Ethiopians (who trace their roots to a supposed union between Solomon and the Queen of Sheba) once had a stake in the Church itself, in these later days they now live in huts on the roof over the chapel of Saint Helena! Every inch of the church is carefully monitored so that no group oversteps its boundaries. Who sweeps what floor, who lights which lamp, who incenses at what hour is all carefully spelled out in detail. If any repairs have to be made, it can take decades for the major groups to agree on a plan. The church in one corner is shimmering in candle light, and in another covered in dust; at one moment its chapels echo with the sound of prayer in countless languages, and in the next the murmurings of tourists reverberate throughout the cavernous interior; its history and shrines make it the most sacred of places, and yet its divisions make it seem almost profane.

I have always found it to be the most difficult church in the world in which to pray. That is until today, the third Sunday of Lent. I had heard that during Lent the Latin Patriarch celebrates Mass on Sunday at 8:30 A.M. in the Latin section of the Basilica called the Chapel of Mary Magdalene. A modern bronze relief of the Risen Jesus appearing to Mary hangs above the altar, just to the right of the tomb of Jesus. I joined two other pilgrims who are staying at Notre Dame, Adrian from the United Kingdom and Cecilia from New York, and we made our way to the Holy Sepulchre to see what the occasion had to offer. In light of past experiences in the Church I was not prepared for what the morning held.

When we arrived the Orthodox liturgy was still being celebrated at the entrance of the Tomb of Jesus and the Coptic Liturgy was being celebrated at the back of his tomb. Waving candles, billowing incense and haunting Eastern chant filled the church. We made our way to the Latin chapel and found seats while we awaited the arrival of the Latin Patriarch. And arrive he did in fine style led by his honor guard and the hammering of their metal-tipped sticks pounding the pavement before him. I had assumed that the liturgy would begin when the Eastern liturgies were completed. But exactly at 8:30 the organ sounded and Mass began. Gregorian chant and Latin incense joined the Eastern rites, and what might, at first, have seemed like dueling of voices soon blended into a hymn of praise.

I was seated facing the altar with the tomb of Jesus directly behind me. As the liturgy proceeded I did not know where to look. I tried to pay attention to the Mass but the chant and bells of Orthodox and Copts vied for my attention. I joined in the Latin and Arabic chant as best I could but I kept looking over my shoulder to see what the other side was doing! I discovered I was not alone. The Franciscan choir seated above the chapel also seemed to keep one eye on their music and one eye on the Greeks! I was afraid I was going to have liturgical whiplash before the Mass was over! But gradually I was able to settle in and savor the richness of traditions surrounding me without being distracted; perhaps because the "distractions" were nothing more than Christians of other traditions solemnly observing Sunday, the day of Resurrection, at the very place where it all began. The most moving part of the ceremony for me, and there were many, was the singing of the Lord's prayer in Arabic and hearing the Father referred to as "Abba," that special title of intimacy that Jesus invited his followers to pray when he taught them the Lord's prayer on a hillside not far from where we were gathered.

When the Mass ended we discovered that the Orthodox liturgy had moved into the section of the Basilica called the Catholicon and was about to end with the grandest procession I have ever seen. The faithful followed servers and priests as they marched three times around the tomb of Jesus before moving outside the church. One of the priests, perhaps it was the Patriarch, carried a relic of the true cross on his head! The Latin rite is known for its "noble simplicity." So what to this Latin-rite priest might, on any other day, have seemed like the strangest of rituals, today blended into the richness of traditions that mark the Church of Jesus Christ.

Cecilia, Adrian and I left the Church of the Holy Sepulchre experiencing sensory overload, and if that was not enough, we turned the corner and met the same man I had photographed a few days ago riding his donkey down the Palm Sunday path on the Mount of Olives!

He greeted me warmly with a kiss on both cheeks and agreed to pose for a picture. He reminded me to stay off the camels! "Jesus rode a donkey," he said, "not a camel!"

The three of us talked of the morning's experience over freshly-squeezed orange juice just across from the Lutheran church of the Redeemer. We all agreed that the liturgical richness of our Church was a gift, a way to express the spiritual reality that lies deep within our hearts: the reality that is the love of a God who gave his only begotten Son that we might have life, and have it to the full (John 10:10). Adrian reminded us of the words of a hymn written by Father Faber that seem most appropriate: Our heart beat fast! We can no more but weep and faint as we adore!

A Morning With Marc Chagall

I spent Wednesday morning at the Hadassah Medical Center in the Ein Karem suburb of Jerusalem. No, I was not sick. I went to visit the hospital synagogue famous for its Chagall stained-glass windows. I had I both studied and taught the windows in Art History classes, but seeing their beauty first hand inspired me and also confirmed the reason they are considered one of the most important works of art in the modern period.

Hadassah, the Women's Zionist Organization of America, is known world-wide for its charitable work. Perhaps nowhere is the fruit of their labor more evident than at the Hadassah-Hebrew University Medical Center. The hospital is a city unto itself, complete with a small shopping mall!

After wandering through a maze of corridors and security I found the synagogue. It is a square, rather modest size room one floor below street level. The windows, depicting the twelve tribes of Israel, are arranged in four groups of three and tower above the synagogue at street level, providing ample light allowing them to shimmer even on cloudiest of days. A recording in English explains the symbolism of each window and also helped me to focus on details easily missed in the array of swirling colors and shapes. I was fortunate that, when the recording ended the five other visitors left the synagogue, I was able to spend time alone meditating and marveling in this most wonderful place where the presence of God is both seen and felt in the genius of Marc Chagall's creation.

Chagall was born in Vitebsk, Byelorussia to a poor Hasidic family. He pays homage to his roots in the "Dan" window by including his small white village house in the midst of a sea of blue. His talent was recognized at an early age. Although it was controversial for a young Jewish boy to become an artist, given the Torah's prohibition against graven images, Chagall was permitted to study in Saint Petersburg. Eventually he made his way to Paris where he lived and worked from 1910 until 1914. The influence of the Cubists, Fauvists and Surrealists artists from that period is quite evident in the geometric shapes, brilliant colors and fanciful, dream-like quality of the windows. When he was approached by Hadassah to design the windows, he accepted the commission without payment and said he felt joy in bringing "my modest gift to the Jewish people, who have always dreamt of biblical love, of friendship and peace among all people... My hope is that I hereby extend my hand to seekers of culture, to poets and to artists among the neighboring peoples."

In light of Chagall's intention it is ironic that the "Issachar" window was destroyed during the 1967 war. When Chagall was notified of the damage he responded by saying "You take care of the war, I will take care of the windows." He provided a new window and included in it a piece of old glass, complete with a bullet hole in the body of the donkey at the bottom of the window.

Chagall's inspiration for depicting the twelve tribes of Israel came from Jacob's final blessings for his sons found at the end of the Book of Genesis (chapter 49) and from Moses' blessing for the twelve tribes found in Deuteronomy 33. The colors he chose represent those describing the breastplate of the High Priest, bejeweled with emeralds, sapphires, jasper, lapis lazuli, turquoise, blue jacinth, agate and beryl. Chagall, steeped in the tragedies and victories of the Jewish people throughout their history, also said that as he was working he "felt my father and mother were looking over my shoulder and behind them were Jews, millions of other vanished Jews of yesterday and a thousand years ago."

One of the blessings I have known in the time I have been in Jerusalem is the opportunity to rediscover the riches of the Jewish Scriptures, what we in the Christian dispensation call the Old Testament. While meditating in the Hadassah synagogue I began to thing about the stories I have read so many times before but now take on new meaning in this place where the actual events took place. While viewing the Temple Mount from the Mount of Olives I have read the story of Abraham's call to sacrifice his son Isaac, since the Holy of Holies was built over the rock where that sacrifice was to take place. While sitting in Gethsemane, at the foot of the Mount of Olives I remember that it was to this same mountain that King David went to mourn over his break with his son Absalom. In the plaza facing the Western Wall I read, as if for the first time, the triumphal story of the building of temple by Solomon and of its tragic destruction by the Babylonians in 587 B.C.

Sometimes I think we only see the Old Testament as preparation for the New. We tend to read the histories, prophecies and psalms in light of the Jesus event. When we do that I think there is a danger of robbing the stories of their richness. We might miss the ways in which the Lord God Yahweh was present to His people, not as a prelude for what was to come later, but in the very moment of their lived experience. That is why the Church encourages us to use the tools of biblical scholarship to understand the world of the Bible, both when the events took place and when they were written down by the inspired writers. We try to understand the trauma of Abraham who heard God's call to leave the security of his homeland and travel to a place unknown, but where God would lead. We imagine the hesitancy of Moses who is commanded to return to the Pharaoh, who sent him into the exile of the desert, with the mission to set God's people free. We identify with the fear in Jesse's heart as his youngest son David is sent forth to do battle with the Philistines in the person of the giant Goliath. And we rejoice with the Jewish people who return from exile in Babylon to rebuild the temple and the holy city of Jerusalem.

Because we are so far removed in time and culture from our Jewish roots, and because our faith took on a decidedly "Roman" identity when Peter moved from Jerusalem to the Eternal City, we have to work hard to reclaim our birthright as children of the promise made to Abraham and his descendants. I think of how often images of Jesus and Mary and other biblical characters have been presented to us as people who appear more European than Semitic. Many of the paintings of the Madonna show a woman who would be more comfortable walking the streets of 16th century Florence than the hill country of first century Judea. Previously I made reference to sixth century mosaics that show Peter dressed as a Senator in imperial Rome, rather than as a fisherman on the shores of the Sea of Galilee. While those images are beautiful and speak to our Western tradition, they do not present a complete picture of our faith heritage, which is decidedly Jewish.

There is a painting at the Notre Dame Center, where I am staying, that speaks to my point. It is an icon of the Holy Family. While Mary and the child Jesus are decidedly Byzantine in appearance, Joseph is shown wearing the tallit, the Jewish prayer shawl. It is an image that is rarely seen, but most appropriate given Joseph's piety rooted in the tradition and dictates of the Law of Moses. It reminds me that Jesus himself must have worn a tallit, since in one of the gospel stories a woman who seeks a cure, reaches out to touch the fringes (tzitzin) of his garment.

A morning with the Chagall windows has helped me to understand how much I treasure these days in David's city that, among other blessings, have once again put me in touch with the richness of our Old Testament biblical history and the wealth of insights to be gained from our Jewish heritage.

"I Like You," He Said

Everyday he comes to the hotel, and everyday he sits in the same chair, at the same table outside the coffee shop where smoking is permitted. Everyday he orders a Maccabee beer. He drinks it and then the waiter brings him a platter from the dining room, the meal of the day.

He says very little. It was only yesterday that I knew he spoke English. I am seated with my laptop at the table opposite his where I can get wireless internet access. He calls to me, "Do you know what time it is?"

"Yes, it is five-thirty."

He pauses for a moment, lights another cigarette, and then says, "I am sorry for bothering you."

"You are not bothering me at all."

"Where are you from?"

"The United States," I answer. "Pennsylvania. Do you know where that is?"

"Pennsylvania? No. I have never been to the United States. I live in Jerusalem. Why did you come here?"

I wonder, how can I explain? "I am a priest on sabbatical. I am here to study, to rest, to pray, to visit."

"And what do you study?"

"The Bible."

"Ah, good. I study the Bible too. The Gospel of John."

"Are you a teacher?"

"No, I am a guide. I study the miracles in the Gospel of John, not for the miracles, but to learn what they mean. Would you like to hear about them?"

As he moves his chair next to mine he asks again, "Are you sure that I am not bothering you?"

"No, not at all. Tell me about the miracles. Tell me about yourself."

"Do you know what is the first miracle in the Gospel of John, the very first?"

"I think it is the wedding feast of Cana in Galilee."

"Yes, it is. You are right! I like you! Do you know what happened? The bride and groom had no more wine. Jesus was there, so he turned their water into wine. That was the miracle. Do you know what happens today when there is no more wine? They call on the telephone and say, 'We need more wine. Send two hundred bottles.' And someone brings more wine. Look at the world today. They do not ask Jesus for more wine. And so look at the world today. That is the meaning of the miracle. We need to ask Jesus for wine. What do you think of that?"

"Tell me your name first."

"It is Louis. I am called Louis."

"Well, Louis, I think it is very interesting. Are you married?"

"Forty-one years! But my heart is breaking. My wife is sick. She is in bed. She cannot move."

"I am sorry to hear that. How did you meet her?"

"She is from Denmark. She came here forty-one years ago on pilgrimage. I was her guide. On the Mount of Olives she saw the golden dome of Saint Mary Magdalene. You know the Church? She said, 'I want to see it.' So I took her there and I told her, 'We have a custom here. You go into a new church and you make a wish.' And when she came out I told her, 'I made a wish too. I wished for you to be my wife.' And four months later I went to Denmark with a ring and we were married. And we are married forty-one years because we asked Jesus for more wine. And now my heart is breaking because she is sick."

"Do you know who were the first pilgrims to Jerusalem?"

I hesitate, and then say, "The three wise men?"

"You are right! I like you! You know what they did? They went to Herod to find Jesus. And Herod said, 'When you find him, come and tell me.' They found Jesus but they did not tell Herod. They went back a different way. That is what you are to do when you come to Jerusalem. You are to go home different. You have people here?"

"There is a group coming next week." "You must tell them about the wise men. Tell them they must go home different. Maybe next time when your group comes I can be your guide."

"Yes, maybe next time."

"Yes, maybe next time. I like you," he says. And then he goes back to his cigarettes. And back to thinking about his wife.

With Simon Peter In Jerusalem

I had forgotten about the beauty of the Church of Saint Peter in Gallicantu and about the strategic land it occupies in the history of Jerusalem, both Old and New Testaments. That is, until I returned there yesterday morning for a visit and a time of prayer. The Church is built on the eastern slope of Mount Zion, the city of David, the forerunner of the city we now call Jerusalem. Looking out from the belvedere, all of salvation history is present before you: the Temple Mount, the Kidron Valley, the Garden of Gethsemane, the Mount of Olives, the Tomb of the Prophets, the road to Jericho, the Hinnom Valley and Aceldema. Yesterday was the perfect spring day to be there. With a blue sky, shining sun, and air as fresh as the morning dew, I was certain the Messiah would reappear any moment!

Some Christians recognize the site as the location of the house of the High Priest Caiaphas, where Jesus was taken after his arrest. There is a deep cistern beneath the church venerated as the place where Jesus was imprisoned on Holy Thursday night (Mark 14:53). Others recognize it as the place where Peter denied Jesus three times (Mark 14:66-72). Ruins on the site of a sixth century monastery and documentation from the same period identify it as the place where Peter went "and wept bitterly" after his denial (Matthew 26:75). Like many of the sites in the Holy Land we will never know for certain which gospel event took place here. But whatever happened here, Peter and his role in the Passion of Jesus is being remembered.

I am struck by the sharp contrast between how Peter is remembered in Rome, and how he is remembered here in Jerusalem. In Rome, Peter is very much the Prince of the Apostles, the "rock" upon whom Jesus built His Church. In sculpture, paintings and mosaics, Peter is presented as more Roman than the Romans. The very size of Saint Peter's Basilica, built over the Apostle's tomb, testifies to the world that he is a figure larger than life. By contrast, the Church of Saint Peter in Gallicantu ("the rooster crowing"), although modern and beautiful, is quite modest in comparison.

I think of my visit to the bronze statue of Saint Peter on February 22, the feast of the Chair of Peter. The statue was dressed in a fine brocade liturgical cope and crowned with a papal tiara. But there is no dressing-up of Peter in Jerusalem, no shining crown. In Jerusalem, he is not Saint Peter; he is Simon bar Jonah, Simon the son of Jonah, the Galilean fisherman. The central image in the Jerusalem Church is an icon of Saint Peter weeping after his denial. It is moving in its simplicity and it evokes in me an identity with the fisherman that seems more true to my nature than the enthroned apostle in princely splendor. History and popular piety want to identify the priest as an "Alter Christus," another Christ. I think most priests see themselves not as Jesus but as the weeping Simon Peter, aware of our shortcomings, yet also overwhelmed by the generous love of a Master, who despite being denied, has enough compassion to return to ask anew, "Do you love me?" (John 21:15)

There is a courtyard outside the Church with a sculpture of Simon Peter speaking the women at the gate who questioned him about his association with Jesus. It presents Peter as outwardly self-assured. However those who know the story are keenly aware that his appearance is deceiving. Even before the cock crowed he must have heard its shrill sound ringing in his ears, echoing louder with each denial that passed his lips. It is easier for me to stand beside the Jerusalem sculpture than the one in Rome, beautiful though it is. It is not because of some exaggerated sense of sinfulness or false modesty; but rather, this statue is a reminder of where the church has come from, from where we were born. It suggests how important that memory is so that we do not lose sight of who we are and what we are called to be.

I am often drawn back to a piece of music that speaks to this awareness. It is Leonard Bernstein's "Mass," a work commissioned for the opening of the Kennedy Center in Washington, D.C. in the early 1970's. It is listed as a theater piece for musicians, singers and dancers. In the opening scene the celebrant takes the stage dressed in blue jeans and a shirt singing the haunting, psalm-like melody "Simple Song." He then dons a simple blue robe. As the "Mass" progresses and the heartaches of people and the complexities of the world are expressed in song and dance, the priest keeps putting on more and more vestments until he can barely stand. In a gesture of great drama, he hurls the sacred vessels to the ground and falls under the weight of his robes. When the stage clears, a young child returns singing the words of the opening number: *"Sing God a simple song, lauda, laude; make it up as you go along, lauda, laude; sing like you like to sing; God loves all simple things; for God is the simplest of all; for God is the simplest of all."*

Maybe it is the freshness of the air, the spring flowers in bloom, or the richness of the biblical setting, but being in Jerusalem calls this pilgrim back, not only to where it all began but also to whom we are in the sight of the Master who lovingly, reassuringly, calls us his friends.

Along the side of the hill next to the Church, there are ruins of an ancient staircase. If the tradition holds that the Upper Room where Jesus celebrated the Last Supper is just up the hill from St. Peter's near the top of Mount Zion, then these are the stairs Jesus and his disciples climbed down on their way to the Garden of Gethsemane. The gospels tell us that after the Passover meal they went out singing songs of praise. Sitting by the stairs, the setting quiet and peaceful, the scent of spring blossoms being carried with the morning breeze, I can almost hear Simon bar Jonah leading the others in song. It is a simple song. Lauda, Laude.

Do You Want To Be Healed? The Pool Of Bethesda And The Church Of Saint Ann

The Gospel for today, Tuesday of the Fourth Week of Lent, tells the story of Jesus healing a crippled man at the Pool of Bethesda (John 5:1-16). So I made my way to the Bethesda Pool to pray and also to visit the Basilica of Saint Anne on the same site. I entered the Old City through Herod's Gate, more modest in appearance than some of the other Gates, but equally beautiful in its simplicity. It leads into the Muslim Quarter of the Old City and, like the other Gates, there are many shops and sellers seeking your attention and business. Just inside the Gate a group of men and women were selling fresh produce. The sights and sounds of the city continue to fascinate me even after being here for nearly a month.

The Gospel story of the Bethesda healing tells us that the Pool was located near the Sheep Gate. Today it is very near Saint Stephen's Gate, also called by its modern Hebrew name, the Lion's Gate. The site is an archeologist's dream come true! Charts and maps outline the centuries of ruins found within a small area. Scholars say that as early as the 8th century B.C. a dam was built here to capture rain water. The area was called the "upper pool" in the Second Book of Kings (18:17) and in the Book of the Prophet Isaiah (7:3). Over the centuries pools were built here and were used as baths for both religious and medicinal purposes. The name "Bethesda" means "House of Mercy," appropriate for a place that was thought of as a healing sanctuary.

In the Gospel story Jesus asked the sick man, "Do you want to be well?" In some ways it is a strange question. Who would not want to be well? And yet, if we think about it, "being well" offers quite a challenge; for "being well" demands being responsible, being industrious, being virtuous, being centered. And above all else, "being well" means living in a manner that both protects and fosters continued healthy living. Perhaps that is why some people seem to "enjoy" poor health! Being well and staying well can be hard work, so perhaps Jesus' question was not so strange after all.

Wellness is a word we often use today to show concern for the well-being of the whole person: body, mind and spirit. Perhaps that is why after healing the man of his bodily illness Jesus tells him, "Look, you are well; do not sin any more, so that nothing worse may happen to you."

Jesus' concern is for the whole person. I think it is significant that the word for "salvation" and the word for "health" come from the same root word "salus." We are "whole" people, and while we speak of body, mind and spirit in order to talk about different aspects of our personhood, the three are inter-related. Did you ever try to pray when you had a toothache? All you can think about is your bad tooth! Or did you ever notice that you seem to be able to think more clearly after going for a walk than after lounging on the couch all day? Maybe that is why we have recess for our school children; letting them exercise and breath in the fresh air before tackling the next math problem or spelling word! Getting enough sleep can be just as important for a healthy spiritual life as choosing the right prayer book. Making time for reflection and prayer not only feeds our spirit, it allows our bodies time for rest and renewal, both essential if we are to have the energy it takes to raise a family, to be responsible at work, or even to enjoy leisure time with family and friends.

I often think that one of the graces of the Sacrament of the Anointing of the Sick is that it allows a person to renew a friendship with the Lord and to put one's spiritual life in balance. When we are reassured of Jesus' friendship and have put our lives in right order, our minds are at ease and our bodies are more receptive to healing and good health. If our spirits languish, our bodies follow. Likewise, when our bodies are tired and our minds are weary, our spiritual life usually suffers as well.

The Pool of Bethesda is next to the Basilica of Saint Anne. The Church was built in 1130 A.D. and I think it is the most beautiful in all of Jerusalem. Tradition holds that this site was the home of Joachim and Anne, the grandparents of Jesus. A cave underneath the church is venerated as the place where Mary was born. Today the Church is cared for by the White Father Missionaries. I met one of the priests, Father Michel LaVoie, who spent thirty five years in the missions and now welcomes pilgrims to this historic, beautiful sight. His warm manner and welcoming spirit convey the serenity we associate with Jesus' gentle, healing presence.

Joachim and Anne must have provided the kind of balanced life for Mary that enabled their daughter to have the "wellness" of body, mind and spirit that not only enabled her to say "yes" to God's plan, but also to have the strength to meet the challenges that "yes" entailed. Today at the Basiica I was fortunate to meet a group of pilgrims from Singapore who were having Mass in the crypt-cave near a beautiful icon of the Nativity of Mary. I joined them for Mass and I prayed for all parents and grandparents who are responsible for providing for the well-being of their children and grandchildren. I also prayed for all us, God's children, God's beloved, that we will be receptive to the many and varied ways our Father calls us to wholeness, to health, to healing.

Joseph The Silent, Joseph The Just

HAPPY FEAST DAY to my dear friends, the faithful of Saint Joseph Parish in Mechanicsburg! Alas, I have not been able to find one church dedicated to Saint Joseph in all of Jerusalem! There is a church dedicated to him in Nazareth, the home of the Holy Family. When I visit there next week I will offer special prayers for all of you. In the mean time, leave it to the Carmelite Sisters to save the day! In their chapel on the Mount of Olives I know there is a shrine to Joseph where I can light a candle and pray for your intentions.

This feast honors Joseph as the husband of Mary. His feast on the first day of May honors him as the patron of workers. I like to think of Joseph as one of the "silent partners" in salvation history, for, indeed he is silent. Not a word of Joseph's is recorded in all of the Scriptures, but like all people of honor and integrity his silence speaks volumes. In business, a silent partner is usually one who invests capital, but who is not part of the day-to-day running of the business. After his dream (Matthew 1:18-25), in which the angel told him not be afraid to take Mary as his wife since it was by the Holy Spirit that she was with child, Joseph invested the capital of his love and faithfulness in caring for Mary and Jesus.

At the age when Jesus would have left the care of his mother and the women of his extended family and been handed over to Joseph for training in a trade and in the ways of Jewish manhood, he announced in the temple that he must be "in his Father's house." Luke tells us that "they did not understand what he said to them," and that "his mother kept all these things in her heart." No doubt Joseph did also.

In Hebrew understanding, the heart is the center of knowledge. Mary and Joseph must have spent many restless nights thinking about what their twelve year old son had said. And at that young age Jesus himself could not have had a complete understanding of his own words for we are told that when he returned to Nazareth with Joseph and Mary, he also had to "increase in wisdom, and age and favor before God and man." (Luke 2: 41-52)

Is it any wonder I love Saint Joseph? For how often in my life does it take time until I begin to understand how the hand of God is at work? So many times after an initial "yes" to God, (like Joseph's agreeing to take Mary as his wife rather then divorcing her quietly) how often am I left pondering in my heart the mysterious plan of God? Saying "yes" to God does not bring understanding; saying "yes" brings the graces needed to wrestle with all the challenges which that "yes" entails. It is in that "wrestling" that I increase in stature of faith so that when I do comprehend, I bow to the wisdom of God, a wisdom beyond my human understanding.

The word the Gospel uses to describe Joseph is "just." One is just who puts things in right order. Joseph put the plan of God first; his own understanding had to wait. Oh for the faith of Joseph! A faith that is just. A faith that is willing to put things in right order. A faith that is willing to wait.

Laetare Sunday Reflections

Once again I decided to spend Sunday morning at the Church of the Holy Sepulchre. But today, Laetare Sunday, I did not go to the Mass celebrated by the Latin Patriarch. Rather, I wanted to "walk around the edges" of the Church as an observer while the liturgy was being celebrated by the different groups who have access to the Holy Sepulchre. Once again it was an enriching experience. I was one of the few visitors in the early morning hours, so in addition to watching and listening to the prayer of the Latins and the Armenians, I was able to visit some of the side chapels of the Basilica without the usual noise and distraction of the crowds.

On the way to the Church I saw the procession of the Latin Patriarch making its way through the streets of the Old City. As he entered the church the Patriarch stopped first to venerate the "Stone of Unction," which is at the foot of Calvary and marks the place where Jesus' body was prepared for burial after the crucifixion. It is located just inside the door of the church and many pilgrims kneel to kiss the Stone at the start of their visit. A large mosaic behind the site shows the body of Jesus being taken down from the cross and placed in the arms of his mother. It also shows his body being prepared for burial before being placed in the tomb, the subject of the thirteenth and fourteenth Stations of the Cross. When the Armenian Patriarch entered the church a few minutes later, he also venerated the Stone.

The Armenian liturgy was celebrated at the tomb of Jesus and the Latin liturgy was celebrated in the chapel of Mary Magdalene, adjacent to the tomb. I went to the Chapel of Calvary and was able to sit quietly and enjoy the blend of the Latin and Armenian chant echoing throughout the Basilica. The only other visitors were the Greek priest who watches over the site and a young woman who was standing in reverent prayer before the ornate altar in the Greek side of Calvary. While praying at Calvary I reflected on today's Gospel, the story of the Prodigal Son and the Loving Father. Unlike the son in the gospel parable, Jesus does not seek independence and the pleasures of this world. Rather, throughout His life he remains in the embrace of His heavenly Father and chooses the way that would lead to his suffering and death. It is in that choice where we find our salvation. The contrast between the two sons, one unnamed and one called Jesus, is stark, but constant is the love and acceptance of both fathers. Whenever I hear or read the opening words of the story, "A man had two sons..." I find myself entering into the reassuring peace that the Father offers when I am willing to "return home" to His loving embrace. In that embrace alone we find true freedom.

I also spent time this morning in the small, cave-like chapel that served as the prison where Jesus and the two thieves who were crucified with him were held. It is not a place many pilgrims find, so even when the church is filled with visitors, the chapel is a refuge. Once again today's gospel comes to mind. Like the Prodigal Son, how often do we find ourselves imprisoned by the delusion that some "thing" or some "place" or some "person" will offer the security and joy we all seek? The words of Saint Augustine come to mind, "Our hearts are restless until they rest in you, O Lord." Only when we rest in Christ do we find the true freedom that allows us to relate to things and places and people not as objects intended for my own satisfaction and security; but rather as gifts given by the Lord that remind me of his gentleness and love.

Around the corner from the Chapel of the Prison a steep stairway leads down to the chapel of Saint Helena and the place where she found the true cross. The site was an abandoned quarry when Helena discovered it in the fourth century. Tombs found nearby give evidence that the site was outside the walls of the city at the time of Jesus, and lend credence to the belief that the place we identify as Calvary and the Tomb of Jesus are indeed the actual sites of the events of Good Friday. It was Helena's piety and determination that led to the building of churches and chapels in Jerusalem and Bethlehem. While our faith is not in places, these sites serve as a touchstone with the historical Jesus and our ancestors in faith who are named in the Bible. I say often that we are "sacramental by nature." We rely on externals to express the deeper inner truths that we live by. Being able to place my hand on the spot where the true cross was found reminds me that the hand of the Risen Jesus is always upon me, guiding me throughout my life's journey. Kissing the stone where the body of Jesus was anointed before burial serves to remind me that I, too, have been anointed in Baptism and Confirmation; not for death but for a life filled with promise and hope because of the dying and rising of Jesus.

Most of what we know in life we learn through our five senses. Being a part of a church that employs those five senses in expressing our beliefs means that faith is more than an idea in our mind, an exercise of the intellect. In the Incarnation we celebrate the "Word becoming flesh," Jesus taking on our human nature. Our sacramental life celebrates that nature as "good" because it has the potential to give life and expression to the profound mysteries that guide our life's journey. There is nowhere like the Church of the Holy Sepulchre, on an early Sunday morning in Lent, that better awakens the senses to the reality of the salvation we know in Jesus, not the Prodigal, but he beloved Son of his heavenly Father. Each new day our Father must rejoice, because this Son of his who was dead has come back to life.

A Day Of Wandering In The Galilee

After seeing the sunrise on the Sea of Galilee it is easy to understand why Jesus found a home here after being rejected in his hometown of Nazareth (Luke 4:16:31). The area still attracts not only religious pilgrims, but people who come here to enjoy the natural beauty of the region; or to "take the cure" in health springs celebrated for their curative powers. Being here at the beginning of the Passover holiday (one week before the actual feast), the city of Tiberias was beginning to fill with families enjoying time away from routine living in a place that invites rest, renewal and relaxation.

On their first full day of pilgrimage, the group from Mechanicsburg, Pennsylvania began their day with a bus ride to the northernmost border of Israel, passing by towns whose names make gospel memories come alive: Capernaum, Bethsaida, Chorozain. In the north, where Israel borders Lebanon and Syria, snow-covered Mount Hermon rises in majesty some 6,000 feet above sea level. Jesus and his disciples came to the foot of the mountain at Caesarea Philipi, one of the sources of the Jordan River flowing into the Sea of Galilee. There he spoke words to Simon Peter that established him as the "rock" upon whom Jesus would build his church (Matthew 16:13-20).

The ruins of a Roman sanctuary to the god Pan (Banias) stand above a visitor's area where the symbolism behind Jesus' choice of words and place becomes obvious. The crystal clear water that flow from the rock foundation of Mount Hermon brings life to all who live along the Jordan River and the Sea of Galilee; so too, the wisdom and grace that will flow from the preaching of Simon Peter (the "rock") will bring the new life and hope of the Gospel message to all who will either hear or inherit the wisdom of his teaching. Jesus intends that Peter's ministry will be of "binding and loosening." As Peter will direct and free on earth, so shall it be in heaven.

It is hard to hear these words and not remember others that Jesus will later direct against the religious leaders of his own day: *The scribes and the Pharisees have taken their seat on the chair of Moses. Therefore, do and observe all things whatsoever they tell you, but do not follow their example. For they preach but they do not practice. They tie up heavy burdens (hard to carry) and lay them on people's shoulders, but they will not life a finger to move them. (Matthew 23:2-4)* How all-encompassing is the authority given to those responsible for preaching the Gospel and directing the life of the church; and how carefully that authority is to be exercised so as not to bruise or break those who are weak and those who struggle.

On the way to Caesarea Philipi we were able to see the town of Rajar, which lies half in Israel and half in Lebanon. Traveling from Caesarea Philipi through Druse villages to Ben Tal, an extinct volcano in the Golan Heights, it was possible to look past the camps of United Nations Peace-Keeping Forces into Syria, Israel's neighbor to the northeast. All the while snow-covered Mount Hermon looms large as the place where the three nations converge. The words of Psalm 133 provided the perfect prayer: *How good it is, how pleasant, where the people dwell as one! Like precious ointment on the head, running down upon the beard, upon the beard of Aaron, upon the collar of his robe. Like dew of Hermon coming down upon the mountains of Zion. There the Lord has lavished blessings, life for evermore.*

After a "Saint Peter's Fish" luncheon on the eastern shore of the Sea of Galilee we made our way across the Lake reading the account of Jesus' quieting the waters after a great storm arose suddenly (Mark 4:35-41). It was difficult to imagine, on this calm sunny day, the forces of nature being so intense that it brought fear a group of experienced fishermen. Yet, it is not so different in life. How often it happens that when life is calm and all is in order we meet our biggest challenges; arising from nowhere, without warning, and with great intensity. At those moments we cry out with the disciples, "Teacher, do you not care if we perish?" Jesus' embarrassing question to his fishermen-disciples challenges us as well. "Why are you afraid," he asked them; "Have you no faith?"

Most of Jesus' public ministry was exercised in this region. To retrace his steps is to be reminded of the power of his message and the assurance of his grace. The blessing of pilgrimage to sacred places is not only to remember events of a time long past; it is to be reminded that the same Risen Lord continues to heal, to teach and to renew his beloved in every age. After his Resurrection we are told that Jesus went ahead of his disciples to Galilee, and so it is with us. The Risen Jesus is always one step ahead of us in our journey through life. Why is it we always seem to want to look back?

Two Villages, Two Women, One Heart

The first two Joyful Mysteries of the Rosary, the Annunciation and the Visitation, belong to Mary of Nazareth and Elizabeth of Ein Karem. Mary and Elizabeth each experienced the Lord's favor, but in very different ways.

In "her old age" Elizabeth found herself to be with child after a lifetime of barrenness, while living with her husband Zechariah, a priest of the division of Abijah. As a young maiden betrothed to Joseph of the house and lineage of David, Mary found herself to be with child through the power of the Holy Spirit. Elizabeth saw in her pregnancy how the Lord had *seen fit to take away my disgrace before others. (Matthew 1:25)* But in the eyes of her people, Mary's pregnancy gave the appearance of unfaithfulness to Joseph, or of indiscretion on both of their parts. Is it any wonder that after the Annunciation by the angel Gabriel, *Mary set out and traveled to the hill country in haste to a town of Judah* to visit her kinswoman Elizabeth? One can only imagine the conversations that took place in Ein Karem during the three months Mary spent with Elizabeth!

Each had a husband who struggled to understand the intervention of God in his life; Zechariah so much so that he was rendered mute during his time of service when selected to burn incense in the temple of the Lord. It was only after his son was born and he insisted that he be named John, as the angel Gabriel has instructed, that Zechariah was able to speak. Obedience to the will of God did not hinder him in any way; rather, he was now free to speak the truth of the God who has visited *and brought redemption to his people. He has raised up a horn for our salvation within the house of David his servant... (Luke*

1:68-69)

Likewise, Joseph did not understand that the hand of God was at work when he discovered that Mary, his betrothed, was with child. It would take the appearance of an angel in a dream to offer the reassurance that Joseph needed to cast aside all fear about taking Mary as his wife. The words of the angel to Joseph speak the meaning of the mystery of the Incarnation: *She will bear a son and you are to name him Jesus, because he will save his people from their sins. (Matthew 1:21)*

I have to believe that Joseph would have accompanied Mary to Ein Karem. No woman would have traveled the road from Nazareth to the hill country of Judea alone. So Zechariah and Joseph would have had their own "visitation" while Mary and Elizabeth offered to each other familial reassurance and spiritual friendship. Unlike the expressive greetings that Mary and Elizabeth offered to one another in the first chapter of Luke's Gospel, we know nothing of the conversation these two men might have had. We can only wonder. Whatever their words, Zechariah, known as being righteous and Joseph, known as being just, eventually followed the way of Elizabeth and Mary and cooperated with God's plan for salvation.

In New Testament times Nazareth was a small village of little consequence. The site on which the Basilica of the Annunciation and the neighboring church of Saint Joseph are located is large enough to have contained the entire village of Nazareth as Mary and Joseph would have known it. Today Nazareth is a bustling, predominately Arab town sprawling over the hillside, visible for miles from the surrounding countryside. We would expect the place of the Annunciation to be the site of a church to commemorate the time and place in history when "the Word became flesh." Had I been the architect, the church would be modest in proportion and humble in appearance to reflect the lowliness of Mary and her docility in the face of God's plan for salvation. Quite the opposite is true. The Basilica stands out in self-conscious splendor in the midst of this rather ordinary Arab town.

Each time I have visited Nazareth I have tried to keep an open mind about the Basilica, but I always leave disappointed. Its interior, its multi-leveled arrangement of chapels, and the oversized, generally ultra-modern depictions of Mary from around the world fail to convey the deep intimacy of the Annunciation. The only exception is the grotto of the Annunciation itself, the actual site commemorating the place of the angel's visit to Mary. Thankfully it is hidden away, apart from the main Basilica on the upper floor. The serenity of the chapel speaks of the deep trust Mary had in her God, Yahweh, and of the deep trust that the Lord God Yahweh had in his handmaiden, Mary. On my recent visit there with pilgrims from Saint Joseph Church in Mechanicsburg, Pennsylvania we were fortunate that there were only a few visitors. In the grotto each person had time for prayer to marvel that God, who is mighty, had done great things for Mary; for indeed, holy is his name.

The Church of the Visitation sits on the slope of a steep hill in the village of Ein Karem. Today Ein Karem is actually a part of the ever-expanding new city of Jerusalem. The ancient village, sitting in a valley beneath the urban sprawl above, maintains an atmosphere of quiet and serenity. It is just the kind of environment that I imagine two women would have needed as they were discovering, together, the dramatic action of God in their lives, while their husbands looked on with amazement. The Church, designed by Antonio Barluzzi, maintains the same reflective character. Its understated architectural style speaks of the gentle strength of these two women of great faith: Mary, who would give birth to Jesus, and Elizabeth, who would give birth to John. Blessed are they who believed that the Lord's words to them would be fulfilled!

The Jordan – More Than A River

Hearing the name of places in the Bible brings to mind mental images of what we imagine them to look like. But when it comes to the River Jordan, erase from you mind any image of a great river like the Mississippi or even the Susquehanna! For most of its meanderings through Galilee, Samaria and Judea, the Jordan is little more than a stream.

To follow the course of the river, from where it begins at the foot Mount Hermon to where it empties into the Dead Sea, is to discover places that played a major role in salvation history, both Old and New Testament.

The source of the River Jordan is a series of streams flowing from the foot of Mount Hermon in the Northern Galilee, where Israel borders Lebanon and Syria. It was here that the tribe of Dan settled when he discovered the fertile soil, rich woodlands and sources of flowing water in the area. We read about it in the Book of Joshua, Chapter 18.

King David also speaks of places in this area in the very moving Psalm 42. In verse 7 David laments: *My soul is downcast within me, therefore I remember thee from the land of the Jordan and Hermon, from the land of Mount Mizar.*

After passing through the Huleh Valley, the Jordan enters into the Sea of Galilee near the ruins of the ancient town of Chorazin. As Jesus was preaching and teaching in the towns and villages around the Sea of Galilee, he chastises Chorazin and Bethsaida for their failure to recognize the wonders he has worked in their midst. His words are chilling: *Woe to you, Chorazin! Woe to you Bethsaida! For if the mighty works done in your midst had been done in Tyre and Sidon, they would have repented long ago in sackcloth and ashes. (Matthew 11:21)*

The Jordan begins again as a river at the southern end of the Sea of

Galilee (also called by its Hebrew name "Gennesaret" in the Gospel of Luke) and flows for sixty-five miles into the Dead Sea. Today the river forms the carefully monitored border between Israel and Lebanon. It is perhaps this area of the Jordan that we most associate with the Scriptures. Somewhere along its southern shores, as the narrow river wanders through the Rift Valley, Joshua led the Israelites and the priests carrying the Ark of the Covenant across the Jordan and entered the Promised Land (Joshua 3).

It is also along this stretch of the river that John was baptizing. Matthew tells us that he preached a baptism of repentance in the desert of Judea, and that many came to hear him and *were baptized by him in the Jordan River as they acknowledged their sins. (Matthew 3:1-17)* In his Gospel, John is a little more specific in his details: *John was also baptizing at Aenon near Salim, because there was an abundance of water there. (John 3:23)*

Throughout the centuries many places, on both the western and eastern banks of the river, have claimed to be the sight where John preached and baptized Jesus. Today the Israeli government has built a park where the Jordan flows from the Sea of Galilee so that pilgrims can safely visit the river, collect water, and conduct baptismal ceremonies.

Just before the Jordan empties into the Dead Sea, the city of Jericho, one of the oldest cities on earth, rests like an oasis along the western side of the river. Today the city is under the control of the Palestinian Authority. High on the cliffs above Jericho is the Mount of Temptations, where, before the start of his public ministry, Jesus entered into prayer for forty days and was tested by the devil.

When the Jordan finally ends its course it has descended from 675 feet below sea level in the Galilee, to 1300 feet below sea level at the Dead Sea, the lowest place on earth. The Dead Sea has a solid chemical matter of twenty-seven per cent. It has a heavy concentration of salt because it has no outlet.

I have come to see the Jordan as more than a river; it is a metaphor for my life. As the Jordan begins its life with the fresh, clear waters from Mount Hermon, I begin my life in the living waters of Baptism. I also meander through life, and like the river, walk a middle-ground trying not to cross the borders that are the excesses of life. In our Catholic tradition we call this path the way of virtue. I know that if my life is lived selfishly, without charity and giving, I will dry up like the Dead Sea. When I find no outlet to share what I have been freely given by the good and gracious Lord, no life will be found in me.

The prophet Ezekiel had a vision describing what we would call the life-giving power of God's amazing grace. In the prophet's vision, new life comes to the Dead Sea.

Then he brought me back to the entrance of the temple, and I saw water flowing out from beneath the threshold of the temple toward the east, for the façade of the temple was toward the east... Then he brought me to the bank of the river, where he had me sit. Along the banks of the river I saw very many trees on both sides. He said to me, "This water flows into the eastern district down upon the Arabah, and empties into the sea, the salt waters, which it makes fresh. (Ezekiel 47)

In the Gospel of John, Jesus speaks about the temple being destroyed and being built up again in three days (John 2:13-22). The evangelist tells us that he was *speaking about the temple of his body. Therefore, when he was raised from the dead, his disciples remembered that he has said this...*

In the Easter sesaon, we rejoice that as water and blood flowed from Jesus' side as He hung upon the cross, we have been renewed in the waters of Baptism and nourished in the Eucharist, the Body of Christ. Like the Dead Sea refreshed by the water flowing forth from the temple in Ezekiel's vision, we have been given new life and flow like the Jordan, a river whose waters were made holy by Him whose vision was our salvation.

The Hopes And Fears Of All The Years Are Met In Thee Tonight

In those days a decree went out from Caesar Augustus that the whole world should be enrolled. This was the first enrollment, when Quirinius was governor of Syria. So all went to be enrolled, each to his own town. And Joseph too went up from Galilee from the town of Nazareth to Judea, to the city of David that is called Bethlehem, because he was of the house and family of David, to be enrolled with Mary, his betrothed, who was with child. While they were there, the time came for her to have her child, and she gave birth to her firstborn son. She wrapped him in swaddling clothes and laid him in a manger, because there was no room for them in the inn. (Luke 2:1-7)

It seems out of season to be writing about Bethlehem in March. In our spiritual sensibilities it is a town that belongs to the winter - to frozen midnights, when brilliant stars in crystal clear heavens shine on the darkened earth below; an earth frozen and waiting; an earth longing for peace. Here in the Holy Land, places significant in our faith history cannot be held captive by a date on a calendar, by a human reckoning of time. Bethlehem, Gethsemane, Nazareth – they belong to all times, to every season. When I visited here as a student over thirty years ago, I still remember walking the Via Dolorosa (the Way of the Cross) in the afternoon and then spending that evening, Christmas eve, in Bethlehem. And fittingly enough, because there is only one mystery with many manifestations: the mystery of God's love revealed throughout the ages to prophets and kings, shepherds and wise men; a love revealed most fully in the birth of his Son Jesus, who would save his people from darkness and despair by his suffering, death and resurrection.

In the fourth century the emperor Constantine built three churches in the Holy Land, each one over a cave. The Eleona Church on the Mount of Olives was built over the cave commemorated as the sight where Jesus, in secret, revealed to His disciples the mysteries of his kingdom; where he taught them the Lord's Prayer; and where he ascended into heaven. The Church of the Holy Sepulchre was built over the cave that served as the tomb of Jesus. The Church of the Nativity was built over the cave where Mary gave birth to her first born son, because there was no room for them in the inn.

As is the case with many places in Israel these days, travel to Bethlehem is more complex because it lies within the Palestinian territory, behind the wall, or as the Israeli government describes it, "the security fence." There is a check point at the entrance to the city where during a visit a few weeks ago, Mechanicsburg pilgrims transferred from an Israeli bus with an Israeli guide to a Palestinian bus with a Palestinian guide, all within sight of the banner of the Ministry of Tourism proclaiming "peace be with you." Once the transfer was made we were welcomed by our guide to Bethlehem which, he told us, we as Christians could call our home, because it was here that Jesus was born.

Over the years Bethlehem has become a largely Muslim town. Many of the Christian families who lived here for centuries have left, some moving abroad because life for in this city has been anything but peaceful. It is a testimony to their faith that those who have remained try to maintain a Christian presence in the face of great opposition. They provide a welcoming spirit to those who come to venerate the places we read about in the second chapter of Luke's gospel; places we associate with "silent stars" and "everlasting light."

From the exterior, the Basilica of the Nativity does not have much to recommend it. Visitors enter the church through a low, narrow entrance way, said to be constructed this way to prevent Crusaders from entering the church on horseback. Centuries of wear, in evidence everywhere you look, testify to the long, sometimes tumultuous history of the site, claimed by some to be the longest continuously used Christian Church in history. Floor mosaics, from the fourth century church of Constantine, are visible beneath the current level of the Basilica. In an odd convergence of the ancient devotion and modern decoration, Christmas balls hang from votive lanterns throughout the nave of the Church.

The focus of the Church, indeed, its very reason for being, is the grotto of the Nativity underneath the sanctuary. A steep, narrow stairway leads pilgrims to the site venerated as the birthplace of Jesus. At once common yet sublime, the intimacy of the grotto offers visitors a sense of belonging, a feeling of welcome. Though it is impossible for the mind to comprehend the mystery of the Word becoming Flesh, kneeling to kiss the star beneath the altar, the heart understands instantly. Here, in this place, God became one like us and from that moment on we have never been the same. Here, in this place, a new Adam was born of a new Eve. Here, in this place, centuries of disobedience and mistrust gave way to a new era of faithfulness and renewed hope that will see the world through until the end of time as we know it.

Now there were shepherds in that region, living in the fields and keeping the night watch over their flock. The angel of the Lord appeared to them and the glory of the Lord shone around them, and they were struck with great fear. The angel said to them, "Do not be afraid; for behold, I proclaim to you good news of great joy that will be for all the people. For today in the city of David a savior has been born for you who is Messiah and Lord. And this will be a sign for you: you will find an infant wrapped in swaddling clothes and lying in a manger." And suddenly there was a multitude of the heavenly host with the angel, praising God and saying: "Glory to God in the highest and on earth peace to those on whom his favor rests." (Luke 2:8-14)

One has a sense of being at home in the Shepherd's Field. Celebrating the Mass of Midnight in the Cave, proclaiming the Christmas Gospel, and singing Silent Night in March did not seem "out of season" at all. So far reaching is the meaning of the Incarnation that it resonates with each day, with every moment of our lives. The Ethiopian Monks who live on the roof of the Church of the Holy Sepulchre seem to understand this better than most. They celebrate Christmas one day every month! Perhaps that is why they seem to be the most serene of all the Christian clerics who lay claim to that place.

The Church in the Shepherd's Field is another masterful work by Antonio Barluzzi. Intending to design places that speak the meaning of the events they commemorate, he designed this church to look like a Bedouin tent. The tent speaks not only of the transient life of the shepherd; but is a reminder to all who visit that, in this life, we have no permanent dwelling.

The paintings in the church have a storybook quality about them. They tell the story of shepherds who move from great fear to great rejoicing; from minds that do not comprehend what they have seen to hearts overflowing with praise for what has been revealed to them. How appropriate then, that in this city of David (the shepherd boy who would become King of Judah) it was a band of shepherds who would be the first to hear the good news of the birth of a new King who would rule forever.

Just as it is difficult each year to see the Christmas season come to a close, it is never easy to leave Bethlehem. The hope is that we take its meaning and message, its spirit and hope with us as we make our way and return to the business of everyday living. As my new Jerusalem friend Louis often reminds me, like the Wise Men we are to return home a new way; we are to return home changed by the experience. So we leave Bethlehem with a prayer, as the Prince of Peace intended, that the walls that divide peoples and nations and families will crumble under the weight of love bestowed on humanity when the Word became Flesh, and dwelled among us.

O Little Town of Bethlehem, how still we see thee lie; above thy deep and dreamless sleep the silent stars go by. Yet in they dark streets shineth, the everlasting light. The hopes and fears of all the years are met in thee tonight.

Preparing For Holy Week
In Jerusalem

There is a felt anticipation throughout the city of Jerusalem as thousands of pilgrims begin arriving for the celebration of Passover and Holy Week.

In the Christian quarter palms are braided and olive branches gathered in preparation for the solemn procession on the Mount of Olives on Sunday afternoon. The faithful will walk from the village of Bethpage to the Old City in remembrance of the Lord's triumphal entry "into his own city" as the introduction to the Mass that day reminds us.

In the Jewish Quarter extensive cleaning of every inch of house and car prepares for the solemn observance the feast of deliverance, remembering when the angel of death passed over the house of the Israelites living the last night of their enslavement in Egypt. For the Jewish people throughout the world, beginning at sunset on Monday, it will be a night that is different from every other night. For this pilgrim in Jerusalem it is hard to imagine what the week will bring.

The schedule of Holy Week liturgies being celebrated throughout the city is as complex as the battle plan of any general about to go to war. With the variety of traditions and expressions within the Christian world, and with major tensions and divisions among those groups, doors to holy places will open and close numerous times each day of Holy Week so that the liturgical rituals of each group can be accommodated. The complexity makes for some awkward scheduling. For example, the Latin Rite Easter Vigil at the Church of the Holy Sepulchre is celebrated on Holy Saturday morning. There are numerous Palm Sunday processions beginning early Sunday morning and lasting throughout the day. The billowing smoke from one incense burner barely has time to clear before the liturgy of the next Rite begins.

Tickets for some liturgical celebration are required for admittance through security barriers. Israeli police and military work to keep the peace as the followers of Jesus jealously vie for time and turf in the holy places throughout the city. The colors of liturgical vestments will be rich and varied. These divisions within Christendom ought to cause all of those responsible for that division to blush red with shame. I wonder why Latin Catholics, Greek Orthodox, Armenians, Copts, Syrians and Ethiopians are not able to walk the Palm Sunday route of Jesus together, since each places its hope for salvation in the suffering, death and resurrection of the same High Priest. One can imagine the first Palm Sunday with Jesus finishing his first entry into the city, only to repeat it many times over so that each group calling itself his disciples would be satisfied! Have we forgotten that the night before he died Jesus prayed "that all may be one?"

On Friday afternoon the group of pilgrims visiting from Mechanicsburg prayed the Stations of the Cross while walking along the Via Dolorosa. It was a moving experience that in many ways reflects the challenges we encounter everyday in trying to live the Christian life. While moving from Station to Station vendors continued to try to lure pilgrims into their shops, "not to buy, just to look." The noise of the city did not stop because a group of pilgrims was trying to pray. Just as in everyday life, distractions were everywhere. Staying attentive and being prayerful were hard work! When we arrived at the tomb of Jesus to pray the fourteenth station, the Greek Orthodox priest responsible for welcoming pilgrims into the tomb pushed and pulled, jostled and tugged, scolded and yelled at good people simply trying to be prayerful. He proved to be more distracting than any street vendor. They, after all, were trying to sell a postcard in order to make a living. He, on the other hand, whose work was to offer a glimpse of the resurrection at the place where it all began two thousand years ago, blurred the good news with a condescending attitude and disrespect that would rightly earn him the title "tomb-nazi."

I can only marvel at the faith of good people who overlooked the disrespect shown to them and concentrated instead on the wonder of the empty tomb and its invitation to live free from fear and sin and death. Perhaps that is what Holy Week is all about: seeing beyond the all too obvious imperfections of the human condition and living, if only for a moment, in the hope that is the promise of Easter.

Palm Sunday In Jerusalem

The Children of Jerusalem welcomed Christ the King. They carried olive branches and loudly praised the Lord: Hosanna in the highest!

On Palm Sunday afternoon people from the world over make their way to Bethpage on the eastern slope of the Mount of Olives. While palm branches wave and singing fills the air, thousands of pilgrims process down the western slope of the mountain following the path that Jesus took when he entered the Holy City to the acclaim of the crowd. In a city that is often somber and watchful, the mood today is decidedly festive. The crowd is friendly and joyful, but also solemn and prayerful. Those in procession do not seem to notice the presence of so many Israeli security personnel, whose numbers seem excessive and whose demeanor betrays boredom.

The crowd is made up of clergy and religious sporting every imaginable style of habit. But their vesture is overshadowed by the colorful Scout Troops marching in line. There is even a Catholic Arab Scout Troop whose drummers and bagpipers are a match for any heard in a Saint Patrick's Day Parade. As the procession winds its way past the gate of the Church of Saint Mary Magdalene, the Russian clergy and their wives keep a watchful eye, appearing not to know whether to applaud or close the gate.

I pause as we pass the domes of the Church of All Nations in the Garden of Gethsemane. Suddenly my mood seems more subdued; the domes of the Church serve as a reminder of what will follow, in a few short days, when Jesus rides not in triumph, but rather lies prostrate in prayer, his soul sorrowful even unto death. From Gethsemane, the Eastern Gate of the Temple is visible. It was probably through these gates that Jesus entered the city, but they have been closed for centuries. A prophetic tradition has them reopened only when the

Messiah returns in triumph to claim Jerusalem once again as his own.

Proceeding up the hill toward Temple Mount we enter the city through the Lion's Gate. The words of Psalm 24 come to mind: *Lift up your heads, O gates; rise up, you ancient portals, that the king of glory may enter.* The gate shows damage from the 1948 War of Independence and the 1967 Six Day War; but the memory of war seems out of place today as those perched above the gate wave palm branches that lay claim to a different kind of freedom, the freedom that belongs to the children of God. Again the words of Psalm 24 seem appropriate to the spirit of the day: *Who is the King of glory? He is God the mighty Lord! Hosanna in the highest! Blessed are you who have come to us so rich in love and mercy! Hosanna in the highest!*

Entering the gate I see a Moslem woman watching closely from her window above the street. Several times she moves away only to come back again. Like the Russians on the Mount of Olives, she seems unsure about her response. As we pass the Church of Saint Anne, the birthplace of Mary, the festive mood is challenged by the call to prayer from the neighborhood Mosque. It is a sobering reminder that in the numbers game in this city, Christianity comes in a distant third.

But for today those in the number one and number two spot, Jews and Moslems respectively, look on with weary eyes as the Christians of the Holy City have their day in the spotlight. On this Palm Sunday, with great fervor and conviction, they wear their faith not only on their sleeves but also on their faces filled with joy and hope. And in a city that is always rife with tension and uncertainty, that joy and hope has much to offer.

Monday Of Holy Week With Mary Of Bethany

This morning I attended the 8:00 Solemn Mass at the Church of the Holy Sepulchre. The Franciscans celebrated the Mass at the Tomb of Jesus. I had hoped to have quiet time for prayer early in the day before large numbers of pilgrims arrived to visit the Church on this Monday of Holy Week. A few Franciscans led the Latin chant and only a small number of the faithful were in attendance, so the mood was prayerful in a church that is usually punctuated by one distraction following another.

The Liturgy of the Word was celebrated in front of the tomb, and then the celebrant entered the inner chamber of the tomb for the Liturgy of the Eucharist. Sitting outside the tomb and hearing the Eucharistic Prayer being chanted inside two rooms away created a mood for me that was both solemn and strange. My preference would certainly have been to be able to see, not just hear the celebrant praying with the faithful present. However, given the unique configuration of the tomb and the complexities created by the divisive politics of this particular Church, the arrangement this morning was the best one could hope for and did lend itself to prayer in this, the most holy of sites in all of Christendom.

The Gospel for Monday of Holy Week (John 12:1-11) tells the story of Mary of Bethany anointing the feet of Jesus with "costly ointment of pure nard." While she dries the feet of Jesus with her hair, her sister Martha serves those present as their brother Lazarus, raised from the tomb, reclines at table with Jesus.

Throughout the centuries the Church has resisted attempts to harmonize the four gospels into one. Each gospel tells the story of Jesus from the unique point of view of the particular evangelist being read. Any attempt to blend the stories together would blur that perspective and much would be lost. Even so, it is hard to hear this gospel and not think of the story told by Luke (10:38-42). In a much treasured passage, Luke tells us that Martha was "distracted by much serving" while Mary "sat at the Lord's feet and listened to his teaching." Although the details of their accounts are different, John and Luke present portraits of Martha and Mary that are complimentary.

When remembered after the experience of the death and resurrection of Jesus, Mary's anointing the feet of Jesus is seen as a prophetic action. For in a few short days the lifeless body of Jesus would be anointed for burial after being taken down from the cross. When Judas raises objection to what he considers the extravagance of her actions, Jesus affirms the foreshadowing signified by Mary's gesture signifies when he says, "Leave her alone. Let her keep this for the day of my burial."

During this Holy Week I am invited to remember the events of the final act in the drama of Jesus' Passion and Death in order to discover what meaning those events have in my own journey of faith. Today, Mary provides me with some direction. Her close friendship with Jesus led her to anoint his feet in anticipation of his burial. In the friendships that I enjoy and in the life I share with all of God's children, I am to anoint others in anticipation of their burial. That is, I am called to affirm all that is holy within them; believing that affirmation will offer renewed reassurance that God, who began the good work within them, will bring it to fulfillment when their life's journey has ended. Perhaps that is the most important work we do as disciples of Jesus. Perhaps that is what He intended when he preached the Sermon on the Mount. Perhaps that what lies at the heart of the two great commandments, love of God and love of neighbor.

In a world that seems to thrive on competition, in a world where success depends on getting the upper hand and securing the leading edge, I am called not to compete but to compliment; not to assail but to affirm; not to annihilate but to anoint. At the beginning of this week of grace and blessing, it is Mary of Bethany who has given me an example. As she has done, I also must do.

Reading Matthew At The Western Wall On The Tuesday Of Holy Week And The First Day Of Passover

A fourth century pilgrim to Jerusalem named Egeria tells us in her diary that on Tuesday of Holy Week the Bishop of Jerusalem read chapters 24 and 25 of Matthew's Gospel at the Eleona Church on the Mount of Olives. The church was built over a cave where it was believed that Jesus taught his disciples in secret. I thought I would read those same chapters today but at a different location.

On this, the first full day of the Passover holiday, I wanted to pray at the Western Wall. As I made my way to the Wall through the Armenian and Jewish Quarter of the Old City, it was obvious that today was a holiday of great importance. As happens on Shabbat, all stores and services in the Jewish sections of the city are closed. There is no bus service and, in the Jewish Quarter of the Old City, the only movement was a rush of people on their way to pray at the Wall. Jews in every manner of garb were present at the Wall in numbers greater than any other day I had visited. The calm and quiet reminded me of Sundays when I was a boy. Long before shopping malls were open seven days a week, at a time when the command to observe Sabbath rest was taken seriously, the routine of life was broken for a day and time spent relaxing with family and friends was the only serious business conducted on Sunday. That same feeling of renewal and abandonment was in the air today throughout the city as the Jewish people remembered why this day is different from every other day.

When I finished praying I sat on a bench a short distance from the Wall and read what Jesus had to say to his disciples in Matthew 24 and 25. After his triumphal entry into Jerusalem and after offering a somewhat stinging indictment of the Pharisees and Sadducees in the temple area, Jesus went with his disciples to the Mount of Olives (Egeria's cave?) and began to teach them privately. These two chapters of Matthew serve as Jesus' final testament shared with those closest to him.

The Western Wall was actually a retaining wall built against the Temple Mount during the time of King Solomon. One story tells of angels being sent to the Wall during the destruction of the temple by the Romans in 70 A.D. It is said that their tears kept the flames away from the wall and that angels will continue to weep there until the temple is rebuilt. It was sobering to face the Wall and read these words of Jesus: *Amen, I say to you, there will not be left here a stone upon another stone that will not be thrown down. (Matthew 24:2)*

The two chapters of Matthew proper to this Tuesday of Holy Week are sometimes called the "apocalyptic" sermon of Jesus, his teaching about the end times. Perhaps the words that are most familiar to us are those describing the scene of the final judgment (Matthew 25:31-46). Jesus tells his disciple that it is the practice of the Corporal Works of Mercy that will serve as the criterion for entrance into the kingdom. The words that most captured my attention today were those spoken by Jesus when he described a time of "wars and rumors of war" and then warned about false prophets who will rise up in his name and try to lead people astray. Jesus said: *Because of the increase of evildoing, the love of many will grow cold. (Matthew 24:12)*

I know I have read those words many times before, but only today, in this sacred place during this holy week is their meaning so apparent. When faced with conflict and challenge, when victimized by evil and oppression, how easy it is to set love and forgiveness aside while our hearts grow cold with bitterness and resentment.

I am reminded of my visit to the Galilee and the Mount of the Beatitudes. While sitting on the side of the hill, the sun shining and the blue sky offering a sense of calm and a promise of peace, it was easy to hear the challenge of the Sermon on the Mount and give assent to the blessedness of the meek, the merciful and the pure of heart. But when push comes to shove and the sun is no longer shining and the blue of the sky gives way to clouds of uncertainty and injustice, Jesus' warning rings true. When wickedness is multiplied, how easy it is for my love to grow cold.

Perhaps that is why we need a Holy Week each year; a time to remember that it is in the course of "real living" that the challenge of the Gospel is realized. Jesus himself will provide the example we need on Holy Thursday evening in the Garden of Gethsemane and on Good Friday on the hill called Calvary. When faced with his impending arrest and crucifixion, he does not allow his love to grow cold. "Put your sword back into its place," he will tell Simon Peter, "for all who take the sword will perish by the sword." While looking at his executioners from the throne of the cross, he will render an order that does not to seek revenge; but rather he will pray, "Father, forgive them; for they know not what they do."

When Jesus predicted his impending death Simon Peter told him that he would stand by him and go wherever he would go. And all the other disciples agreed. But Jesus warned Simon that before the cock would crow, he would deny him three times. Simon Peter and the other disciples had first to experience the Resurrection of Jesus before being able to follow in his footsteps. Saint Paul understood this as well and that is why he prayed that he might know Christ "and the power of his resurrection." (Philippians 3:30) That is why we do not lose hope as we walk with Jesus to the cross during this Holy Week. For we who have been baptized into his death and have been buried with him, shall also share in a like resurrection.

Wednesday Of Holy Week – Singing Of The Passion And Veneration Of The Column Of The Flagellation

Each day of Holy Week in Jerusalem has different liturgical offerings at the sites that hold special meaning in the Passion of Jesus. In the morning there is a Solemn Mass celebrated by the Franciscans in the Church of the Holy Sepulchre. At that Mass this morning there was a special offering – the Passion of Mark was chanted in Latin by three priests standing before the Tomb of Jesus. It was quite moving to hear the leader sing of Joseph of Arimathea: *Having brought a linen cloth, he took him down, wrapped him in the linen cloth and laid him in a tomb that had been hewn out of the rock. Then he rolled a stone against the entrance of the tomb.*

After the Mass the Franciscan chapel was opened and the faithful were invited to venerate the column of the flagellation, a relic associated with the sorrowful mystery of the Scourging at the Pillar. With great devotion young and old alike climbed five stairs and kissed the column. The experience, once again, reminded me of how important signs and symbols are to us in our Catholic faith. Many times during my stay in Rome, and now here in Jerusalem, places and objects representative of the mysteries of our faith give expression to the unseen reality of God's saving grace. It is not that my faith is in a column, or a stone, or even an empty tomb. Rather, these things feed my senses and remind me that faith is not just an idea in my mind; it is a living reality given ultimate expression in Jesus becoming one like me, the Word became Flesh. Just as I seek to express friendship with a bouquet of flowers or a special gift, so too I express my faith using signs, symbols and gestures that speak the meaning of all that I hold to be true.

I am reminded of a story about a young woman who moved away

from home and telephoned her mother faithfully every week. One day her mother complained that her daughter never sent her a letter. "But I call you every week," her daughter answered in her own defense. "Yes, I know," responded the mother, "but I cannot put a telephone call under my pillow."

The liturgies of Holy Week are filled with meaningful signs and symbols: the aroma of incense and the sight of our prayers rising to God; the kissing of the cross at the Good Friday commemorating the Lord's Passion; the sprinkling with holy water during the renewal of our baptismal promises at Easter Mass. These signs and rituals have come down to us throughout the ages and, for centuries, have been the way our faith finds expression employing all five senses.

Our culture often struggles to find common symbols that give expression to shared values and beliefs. One need only think of the frustration and bitterness often expressed by families of the victims of the September 11 tragedy as artists presented ideas for a memorial to their loved ones. The pain and loss suffered by so many was a shared reality. Finding ways to express those feelings proved to be difficult in a society that is often stoic and literal in its approach to life.

In the earthly ministry of Jesus, signs often accompanied his words and his teachings. He spat on the ground and made a paste, rubbing it on a blind man's eyes that he might see; he placed his fingers in the ears of a deaf man and he was able to hear; he performed the first of his signs at a wedding at Cana in Galilee and provided for a newly married couple the water made wine. Jesus knew we are a people who learn best by seeing and by touching. He understood that we are "sacramental" by nature. So from the beginning, his disciples have followed his example and have used signs and symbols to express the wonders of our faith and the saving grace given to us by the Risen Lord.

The mystery of salvation we know in the suffering, death and rising of Jesus may be beyond our comprehension. But our ability to express that mystery, in sign and symbol, keeps its meaning ever before our eyes as we reach out to touch the God whose will is our salvation.

Holy Thursday In Jerusalem

I have always found the Mass of the Lord's Supper celebrated on Holy Thursday evening to be one of the most meaningful liturgies of the entire Liturgical Year. As the Second Vatican Council reminded us, the Mass is at the heart of our Catholic Christian spirituality, the "source and summit" of the Christian life. To remember the Last Supper, when Jesus gave himself to us in the gift of the Eucharist, is to go back to the beginning of our sacramental life. While being in Jerusalem for Holy Thursday is a blessing, it also brings with it a feeling of disappointment. The "Upper Room," venerated as the place where Jesus celebrated the Passover Supper with his disciples, is not used for liturgical celebrations. Since it has been under the control of the Israeli government it is more accessible to pilgrims than it had been in previous years. But still, no Mass is celebrated in this special place on Holy Thursday or any other day of the year. The only exception was in 2000 when Pope John Paul II celebrated Mass there with twelve concelebrating bishops as part of his pilgrimage during the Jubilee Year.

Although there is a procession to the site in the afternoon, one has to look elsewhere for the celebration of the Holy Thursday Mass of the Lord's Supper. On this morning I concelebrated the 8:30 Mass at the Church of the Holy Sepulchre with the Latin Patriarch, Michel Sabbah, serving as main celebrant. He was joined by five other bishops and about 125 priests from all over the world. The early hour was necessary to accommodate the different groups (Latin, Orthodox, Armenian, Coptic, Syrian and Ethiopian) who all lay claim to the Church. The program explains it this way: "This Mass is usually celebrated in the evening, however due to the local situation here in Jerusalem, it is anticipated and celebrated in the morning." Since we remember the Mass not only as the banquet of the Last Supper but also as the sacrifice of Calvary, being just a few yards from the place of the Crucifixion helped me to reconcile the disappointment I felt about the Upper Room being off limits for worship on this most holy day.

The three hour liturgy combined the Mass of the Lord's Supper and the Mass of the Oils. The priests who were present renewed their priestly commitment and the Holy Oils were blessed. The Patriarch washed the feet of twelve Franciscans and at the end of the Mass led a very moving, candle light procession with the Blessed Sacrament encircling the Tomb of Jesus three times. The third time around the priests and Patriarch Sabbah walked to the Stone of Unction where the body of Jesus was prepared for burial and then the Patriarch placed the Blessed Sacrament in the Tomb. The program note explains: "In the tomb, a tabernacle has already been prepared and therein is placed the Lord's Body in the form of bread. Christ is only resting here, for as we know, He is risen as He promised. He is our spiritual food and drink and, in the action of receiving Him, He remains alive in our hearts and in the sacrifice of our prayer and praise."

The Mass was solemn, prayerful and sung entirely in Latin with the homily delivered by Patriarch Sabbah. The 120 page Mass program was most helpful since it provided translations in Arabic, Italian, English, French, German and Spanish. The homily was delivered by the Patriarch in French. Since I so not know the language I used that time for private meditation on the meaning of the Mass as we celebrate it today. I would like to share some of my meditation with you.

During my formative years the Church celebrated the so-called "Tridentine" liturgy. Mass was "said" or "read" by the priest in Latin. His back was to the faithful and, if the church was properly configured, he was facing the East. A "High Mass" meant singing with six candles burning; a "Low Mass" was more subdued with only two candles lighted. The stipend for a "High Mass" was more than for a "Low Mass." The Tridentine liturgy had a solemnity and beauty to it that many still remember with a certain degree of nostalgia.

What I remember most is the careful, almost obsessive attention to detail. Every movement of the celebrant was governed by rubrics, which are directions for the priest printed in red in the sacramentary. Every word and every gesture was carefully noted, with no room for adaptation to the special circumstances of a given celebration. The result was that you could be sure that every celebration of the Mass was just like every one before it, whether you found yourself in Mechanicsburg or Madrid, Camp Hill or Cambodia.

The Second Vatican Council changed all of that when it called for the "full, conscious and active participation" of the faithful present for Mass. It has taken the church some time, but with new translations of the Scriptures better suited to liturgical settings, and new music written by composers who are sensitive both to the importance of meaningful texts, and standards of good music, I think that we have been able to find a balance between what the experts call the horizontal and vertical dimensions of worship; that is between the solemn and the familiar; the Godly and the communal aspects of our common prayer.

There are times at Mass when we are invited to leave behind the routine of our lives and enter into the mystery of our God. This "vertical dimension" of the liturgy raises us beyond the mundane, the ordinary and the limitations of our human condition. The words of Saint Thomas Aquinas come to mind: "Fill us with celestial grace, Thou who feedest us below! Source of all we have or know! Grant with thy saints above, sitting at the feast of love, we may see thee face to face."

There are also times at Mass when we are united with one another in the Eucharist, the bond of perfect charity. This "horizontal dimension" of the liturgy is nowhere better expressed than in the ceremony of the Washing of the Feet when we are reminded that the Eucharist not only unites us with the Lord Jesus, it also invites and challenges us, to enter into communion with one another.

This two-fold dimension of the Mass, the vertical and the horizontal, reflects the tension we know as people made in God's image and likeness, but also as people in need of redemption; people who see Jesus seated at the right hand of the Father, but who also see him in the faces of our brothers and sisters seated next to us at Mass each Sunday.

All of this reminds me that the celebration of Mass is never an escape from everyday living; rather it puts everyday living in right perspective. That perspective was provided by the old catechism when it reminded us that we are made to be happy with God in heaven, but only after we have served him in this life by washing one another's feet.

Today I celebrated Mass for the intention of my brother priests in the Diocese of Harrisburg, and remembered, in a special way those at home who share the Celebration of the Eucharist with me each weekend. Though this year we are miles apart, the same Christ unites us in His love and sustains us with His grace wherever we gather for the Breaking of the Bread until He comes in glory.

Holy Thursday Night In The Garden Of Gethsemane

On this Holy Thursday evening, the Church of All Nations, built around the rock where Jesus prayed in the Garden of Gethsemane, is open until midnight for quiet prayer and reflection. Gethsemane lies at the foot of the Mount of Olives in the Kidron Valley across from the Temple Mount. The olive trees in the Garden are said to grow from shoots of trees dating back to the time of Jesus. Whatever their age, their gnarled appearance set the mood for one of the most dramatic events in the life of Christ. The Gospel of John uses the Garden only as a setting for Jesus' betrayal by Judas and his arrest by *a band of soldiers and guards from the chief priests and the Pharisees. (John 18:1-12)* But Matthew, Mark and Luke tell us that Gethsemane was also a place of prayer for Jesus and his disciples before his arrest, trial and crucifixion. Each gospel writer tells the story, emphasizing a different aspect of the event, and each has something to say to our experience today.

All four Evangelists note that after eating with the disciples in the upper room, Jesus took them to the Mount of Olives. John records that there was a garden there where *Jesus often met with his disciples. (John 18:1)* Matthew highlights Jesus' prayer in the Garden. Each time he returns to find them asleep he instructs them on the need to *Watch and pray that you may not enter into temptation. The spirit is willing,* Jesus warns them, *But the flesh is weak (Matthew 26:41)* Mark, on the other hand, emphasizes the weakness of the disciples and their inability to stay awake. Three times Jesus finds them sleeping, foreshadowing the three denials of Peter a few verses later. Luke reports Jesus praying and returning to the disciples only one time. He is the evangelist who is always gentle with the disciples, understanding their human condition and willing to forgive their weakness. Luke excuses their behavior and tells us that they were *sleeping from grief.* *(Luke 22:45).*

The scene mirrors an event in the life of King David. When he is distraught because his son Absalom has chosen to challenge his authority, *David went up the Mount of Olives and wept without ceasing. His head was covered, and he was walking barefoot. All those who were with him also had their heads covered and were weeping as they went. (2 Samuel 15:30)* Clearly the Mount of Olives is seen as a place for prayer in times of trial.

It is easy to pray in the Church of All Nations. The architect, Antonio Barluzzi, designed it that way. Purple alabaster windows allow only a narrow band of light to flood the church, creating a mood that is both somber and prayerful. The altar, built over the rock where Jesus is said to have prayed *that this cup might pass from me,* is shaped like a chalice. The fencing around the rock is guarded by foreboding ravens and gentle doves, reminding us that as ominous as the time in the Garden was for Jesus, *an angel from heaven appeared to him, strengthening him. (Luke 22:43)*

Mark's account of the Gethsemane story reminds me that being with Jesus in the Garden this night is to acknowledge the presence of forces in our world that keep me from being "watchful and prayerful." It might be all that vies for my attention, draining me of energy so that I am not able to "keep awake" and stay attuned to what is important, what is essential. Or it might be a failure to establish priorities, assigning equal weight to everything that comes my way. It might mean doing good things that need to be done, but in so doing failing to make time for study, for prayer, for rest. In considering the forces that keep me from being watchful and prayerful, the first letter of Saint Peter sets the scene with great drama: *Be sober and vigilant. Your opponent the devil is prowling around like a roaring lion looking for someone to devour. Resist him, steadfast in faith, knowing that your fellow believers throughout the world undergo the same sufferings. (1Peter 5:8-9)*

The Jesus in Gethsemane in Matthew's Gospel is concerned with teaching his disciples about the need to pray. He is concerned when they fall asleep because it means they are not praying. Jesus not only tells the disciples to *watch and pray that you may not undergo the test (Matthew 26:41)*, he shows them the way by praying himself. At the beginning of the account he makes it clear to the disciples why he is there. *Sit here,* he tells them, *While I go over there and pray. (Matthew 26:36)* Only in Matthew's account of Gethsemane does Jesus pray three times. And each time he leaves the disciples to pray, he is able to gradually embrace the will of his heavenly Father. To pray with Jesus in the Garden this night is to hear the call to pray and to be watchful. It is not enough that I live a gospel life; I am also to pray the gospel prayer, *thy will be done. (Matthew 26:42)* Matthew has Jesus, within earshot of the disciples in the Garden, using the same words in Gethsemane that he used when he taught them the Lord's Prayer. Once again we see that, all throughout his ministry, Jesus was preparing his disciples for this night. In the same way he urges me to be prayerful each day of my life so that, in time trial, I might be strengthened.

It is hard not to favor Luke's account of the Gethsemane scene. It is simple and to the point. Jesus prays only one time, and returns to the disciples only once. Luke never wants to show Jesus burdened and filled with grief. He does not want his readers, mostly Gentile converts, to think that Jesus is weak. He is intent on his mission and does not waiver. Luke shows the same conviction on the part of the disciples. He understands their confusion and does not dwell on their weakness, on their falling asleep. He knows that after the resurrection, after the descent of the Holy Spirit, they will have the courage they need to follow Jesus with steadfast heart; and he will tell their story in his Acts of the Apostles. So too with me. Jesus does not leave me orphaned in the Garden. Rather, on Easter Sunday morning an angel will tell the women at the garden tomb, and through them tell me, that *He is not here, but he has been raised. Remember what he said to you while he was still in Galilee, that the Son of Man must be handed over to sinners and be crucified, and rise on the third day. (Luke 24:6-7).* Luke tells us that *they remembered his words.*

And so do I on this most holy night.

Good Friday In The Holy City
A Meditation On The Cross

On this Good Friday in Jerusalem, thousands of Christian pilgrims walk the Via Dolorosa, the way of sorrow, and pray the Stations of the Cross. The stations begin at the site of the Antonia Fortress, the place of Jesus' trial before Pontius Pilate. The procession continues through the old city, stopping along the way to commemorate the final events of Jesus' passion. Business in the city continues at its usual frantic Friday pace. But for the Christian minority of the city, there is nothing routine about this particular Friday. For it is the day we remember the Crucifixion of Jesus and also words to his followers, "If you want to be my disciple, you must take up your cross and follow me."

Of course the focus of today's observance in Jerusalem is Golgotha, the place of the skull, the hill of Calvary in the Church of the Holy Sepulchre. Reflecting the divisions of the church itself, the site of Calvary is divided into two chapels. The Greek Orthodox chapel is directly over the rock of Golgotha and is the site of the twelfth station, Jesus dies on the Cross. The Latin chapel to the right commemorates the eleventh station, Jesus is nailed to the cross.

The Latin chapel is striking in its simplicity. Like many of the holy places in the city it was designed by Antonio Barluzzi. Behind the altar a mosaic depicts the eleventh station with grace and reserve. What might be surprising is that to the right of the altar there is an Old Testament scene, a mosaic of the sacrifice of Isaac, what the Jewish tradition calls the "akedah" or "the binding" of Isaac. Throughout the centuries, the Abraham's sacrifice was seen as prefiguring the crucifixion of Jesus, with one major difference.

God commanded Abraham: *Take your son Isaac, your only one, whom you love, and go the land of Moriah. There you shall offer him up as a holocaust on a height I will point out to you. (Genesis 22:2)* Mount Moriah is the site of the Temple Mount, a short walk from the hill of Calvary. There, God changed his mind and spared Isaac, returning the boy to his father. He provided a ram for the burnt offering sacrifice rather than demanding that Abraham sacrifice his son. On the hill of Calvary the Father did not change his mind; he did not hear the prayer of Jesus in Gethsemane: *Abba, Father, all things are possible to you. Take this cup away from me, but not what I will but what you will. (Mark 14:36)* Rather, the Father God offered his Son, his only Son Jesus, whom he loved, for the salvation of the world. No other sacrifice would do. Only in the sacrificial death of Jesus on the cross could the Father speak to the world the message of His great love for all who are made in his image and likeness.

Often in our Christian piety there is a tendency on Good Friday to highlight the sufferings that Jesus endured during his passion and death. While meditating on those sufferings certainly has much to offer for our reflection, I am reminded of the words of the great scripture scholar, Father Demetrius Dumm, who cautioned, "It is not about how much he suffered; it is about how much he loved." Behind the scourging and the mockery, behind the crowning with thorns and hammering of the nails, there is a story of great love. It is in that great love alone that we find our salvation.

When asked to identify the greatest commandment, Jesus spoke not of sacrifice but of love - love of God and love of neighbor. The Scriptures tells us that Jesus came that we might have life, and have it to the full. When he tells me that, as his disciple, I am to take up my cross and follow him, I believe that he is telling me to embrace the fullness of the life he has given me. And by living that life in love, I will know the cross in the sacrifices and disappointments that often accompany love of God and love of neighbor. I do not have to build my own cross. Simply living life, fully in love, will bring crosses in abundance. It is the great paradox of the Christian life; the greater my response to life in love, the greater my share in the cross of Jesus.

When I embrace the cross as it is manifested in the fullness of my living, I become his faithful disciple.

This morning, as I joined the crowd on the Via Dolorosa, I tried to take Father Demetrius' words to heart. At each station I tried to see the great love behind each person being commemorated, be it Veronica, the women of Jerusalem, or Simon of Cyrene. I was able to find in that love reason to embrace with humility, gratitude and renewed fervor the fullness of life offered by the Jesus on the cross.

Holy Saturday And The Miracle Of The Fire

With an air of excitement and feeling of anticipation that can only be described as electric, thousands of people enter the Old City of Jerusalem on Holy Saturday for the Miracle of the Fire. Some have slept in the streets all night, trying to be at the head of the line when the doors open at the Church of the Holy Sepulchre. Security in the city is heightened. Israeli police and armed military personnel are everywhere. Streets are blocked and the entrances at both the New Gate and Jaffa Gate, those closest to the Church, are carefully monitored. Every age group and every expression of Christianity are represented. The atmosphere is friendly and the mood very celebratory.

Some say the Miracle goes back a thousand years; some say even longer. Whatever its length, the ritual never changes. At 1:30 p.m. on Orthodox Holy Saturday, the Greek Orthodox Patriarch enters the darkened chamber and prays at the tomb of Jesus. He touches a torch to the tomb and a miraculous blue flame lights the torch. In turn, he lights the torch of the Armenian and Coptic Patriarchs and the flame spreads throughout the church and then throughout the city.

Not wanting to fight the crowd and aware that, in past years there have been injuries and even deaths because of the number of people present in the church (there is only one exit), I decided to wait with hundreds of others on the periphery, in the Christian Quarter on Greek Patriarch Street. Many have brought chairs; some wait on the rooftops. Maria's Grocery Store seems to be doing a good business selling water and nut roll. Candle vendors are everywhere; a man with a large copper urn walks through the crowd selling Arabic coffee; cell phones ring; children play and everyone seems to be united in anticipation of the Miracle they are sure will happen once again.

I am standing near one of the bread salesmen who offers a running commentary during the three hour wait. He seems pleased to learn that this is my first time witnessing the Miracle. "Everyone should come here for this," he tells me. "It is only God who can bring people together. Politics can't, but God can," he assures me. "I can tell you something about everyone here. I was born in Jerusalem. See those men over there? They are Egyptian. I can tell just by looking. The woman over there wanted to give me five shekels for a loaf of bread. I tell her I want only one dollar or four shekels. She did not understand me so she walked away. She lost a good deal! Now she is hungry!" The man offers me Arabic coffee (I will probably be up all night!) and continues to entertain me with tales that combine social, political and religious commentary, often in the same sentence. I enjoy his company and his remarks. Somehow I no longer feel like an outsider, like a visitor. That mood is strengthened when some of the waiters from the restaurant who play in the Catholic Arab Scout Band march by. "Father, Abuna!" they call out to me. "Thank you for coming to see us again!" They had played in the procession on the Mount of Olives on Palm Sunday and their greeting that day was just as warm and friendly.

At 2:00 p.m. church bells begin to peal and the excitement starts to grow. Suddenly, from around the corner a block away, a lighted torch appears. Cheers erupt; cameras flash and the crowd is on tip-toe. There is almost a sigh of relief. The tradition continues! The Miracle has happened once again! In seconds the flame makes its way to our location. Some run ahead to be the first to light the candles of those who are blocks away near the entrance of the New Gate.

When I make my way there all of the shops that are owned by Christians have lighted candles in their doorways and on their countertops. They have witnessed the same scene every Holy Saturday of their lives. However for me it is a first, and my eyes are wide-open at the wonder and simplicity of it all. A single flame, whether its source be heavenly or a hoax, for a few moments, at least, is able to unite a city so often rife with tension and suspicion. I enter the shop where I usually buy water and juice. A candle is burning on the counter next to the owner. "Did you see it Father? Did you see it?" "Yes," I answer, "and it was wonderful!" He smiles, but with a puzzled look. "Wonderful? Wonderful? Yes wonderful! That is the word. It was wonderful! Happy Easter to you, Father!"

And already, even though it is Holy Saturday, it is a Happy Easter. The Miracle continues. God has not abandoned his people to the powers of sin and fear and death.

The Evening Of The First Day Of The Week – The Two Disciples On The Road To Emmaus

Now that very day two of them were coming to a village seven miles from Jerusalem called Emmaus, and they were conversing about all the things that had occurred. And it happened that while they were conversing and debating, Jesus himself drew near and walked with them, but their eyes were prevented from recognizing him… Then beginning with Moses and all the prophets, he interpreted to them what referred to him in all the scriptures… And it happened that, while he was with them at table, he took bread, said the blessing, broke it, and gave it to them. With that their eyes were opened and they recognized him, but he vanished from their sight… So they set out at once and returned to Jerusalem where they found gathered the eleven and those with them… Then the two recounted what had taken place on the way and how he was made known to them in the breaking of the bread. (Luke 24:13 passim)

Thank goodness for Saint Luke! After the account of the discovery of the empty tomb he immediately tells his readers how Jesus, risen from the dead, will continue to be present to his followers. Luke tells us that there were two disciples on the road to Emmaus; one called Cleopas, the other unnamed. I like to think the unnamed disciple was Mrs. Cleopas! Their encounter with Jesus that first Easter Sunday night lays the foundation for the Church in the days, weeks and indeed, the centuries that would follow. What a comfort for us to know that, from the beginning, Jesus intended to be present to His followers in the sharing of the word and the breaking of the bread.

That is why for us, disciples of the Risen Lord, Easter is more than a one-day event. Easter lives on whenever and wherever we gather in His name to share Word and Sacrament. Perhaps that is why the Church calls every Sunday a "little Easter" and every Easter the "great Sunday." Like Cleopas and his companion, we are always "on the road" to somewhere; and the same Risen Jesus who opened their hearts to His presence, walks with us as well. When we recognize him, our "hearts burn within us" as we understand the depth of the love of the "Christ," the "anointed one", who gave himself over to death that we might live forever.

The Emmaus story has great meaning for me this year. Not only because I am in Jerusalem on this Easter Sunday evening, only seven miles from that little town; but because I know that, even if I were not here, the same Risen Christ would be present to me wherever I gathered with other believers to share Word and Sacrament in the celebration of the Mass. Certainly I am grateful to be in the very places where Jesus walked and preached, suffered, died and rose again; being here has a special meaning I will always treasure. But I also know that next year, when I am not sailing on the Sea of Galilee on a sunny spring day, or walking down the Mount of Olives on Palm Sunday afternoon, or celebrating the Mass of the Lord's Supper on Holy Thursday at the Empty Tomb, Jesus will be just as present whenever I gather with those who share faith in His name and the power of His resurrection.

At Easter Mass this morning at the Notre Dame Center there were people present from 33 nations. Before each person came to Jerusalem each had already encountered the Risen Jesus, not on the road to Emmaus, but in the specific path of his or her life. Those present had already shared with others how they had come to know him in the "breaking of the bread." For the Risen Lord had already touched their minds and hearts with a felt intensity in Sri Lanka and Holland, Uganda and Mexico, Australia and Ecuador.

I once heard the great priest, teacher and spiritual writer, Henri Nouwen, tell a story about a friend who was sad because he was moving away. In talking about their friendship Father Nouwen said, "I think what has happened is that the Christ in you has recognized the Christ in me; so that now wherever I travel all of the ground between us will be holy ground." Wherever I travel in this world, like the disciples on the road to Emmaus, the Risen Christ walks with me. So that in whatever place I find myself, it is Holy Land.

Easter Tuesday – The Garden Tomb And Mary Magdalene

On this, the third day of Easter, I visited the so-called "Garden Tomb." For centuries questions were raised about whether the Church of the Holy Sepulchre was the actual site of the crucifixion and burial place of Jesus. No one knew for sure the exact location of the ancient city walls. Since tombs had to be located outside the walls, it could not be said, with certainty, that the church marked the exact site of Golgotha and the rock-hewn tomb where the crucified body of Jesus had been placed.

In the nineteenth century, British General Charles Gordon was seated on a rooftop in the Old City and noticed a rock formation in an old quarry just outside the Damascus Gate. To him the formation looked like a skull. He investigated the area and discovered that there were tombs nearby. That property was purchased and Gordon declared that he had discovered the tomb of Jesus. He postulated that Gologtha, the place of the crucifixion, was at the nearby stone quarry he had seen from the old city. It is now the site of a bus station.

Since that time, most archeologists are certain that the location of the Church of the Holy Sepulchre was outside the city walls at the time of Jesus, lending credence to the accuracy of the traditional sites. Also, the dating of the tombs at the Gordon site does not match the time frame of the crucifixion of Jesus. Nevertheless, the Garden Tomb is a quiet, reflective place for meditation. It also provides an alternative for Christians who are not comfortable with the rich liturgical traditions of the six Churches who have possession of the Holy Sepulchre.

Mary Magdalene stood outside the tomb weeping. And as she wept, she bent over into the tomb and saw two angels in white sitting there, one at the head and the one at the feet where the Body of Jesus had been. And they said to her, "Woman, why are you weeping?" She said to them, "They have taken my Lord, and I don't know where they laid him." When she said this, she turned around and saw Jesus there, but did not know it was Jesus. Jesus said to her, "Woman, why are you weeping? Whom are you looking for?" She thought it was the gardener and said to him, "Sir, if you have taken him away, tell me where you laid him, and I will take him." Jesus said to her, "Mary!" She turned and said to him in Hebrew, "Rabbouni," which means Teacher. Jesus said to her, "Stop holding on to me, for I have not yet ascended to the Father. But go to my brothers and tell them, 'I am going to my Father and your Father, to my God and your God.'" Mary went and then reported what he had told her. (John 20:11-18 – Gospel for Tuesday of Easter Week)

The Garden Tomb provides a beautiful setting for reflecting on today's Gospel. Mary had every reason to weep. She had witnessed the trial of Jesus; she had seen him suffer in the darkest hour of his passion; she was standing with the other women at the foot of the cross when he died. As Jesus was buried, Saint Luke tells us that "the women who had come with him from Galilee followed, and saw the tomb." And now, already overcome with profound grief, the thought that the body of Jesus had been taken increased her pain and suffering. Where would she be able to mourn the death of her Lord? In some ways, the question of the angel and of Jesus seems cruel, adding insult to injury. "Why was she weeping?" The reasons were all too obvious; but in forcing Mary to speak the reason for her grief, Jesus touches her at the heart of her pain. Her Lord has died, and now even His body is missing.

When Jesus speaks her name and she recognizes Him, His teaching about the Good Shepherd comes to life: "The sheep hear his voice, and he calls his own sheep by name" (John 10:3). When Mary answered Jesus' question, her pain identified her as a woman who was lost. Only in her loss would she be able to hear Jesus' voice, for He came to seek out those who were lost.

Jesus' words to Mary, "Stop holding on to me, for I have not yet ascended to the Father," are very telling. Mary's experience was of the earthly Jesus. Now that Jesus is no longer of this world, Mary has to change her way of thinking about Him. She knew Him as Jesus, the itinerant preacher from Nazareth. Now she will know Him as Jesus, the Son of God. Mary's experience of the earthly Jesus and her thinking of Him in human terms limit the power of his resurrection. Just as on the cross Jesus opened his arms and embraced the world, Mary must now open her mind and heart to embrace all that Jesus, the Risen One, has to offer those who are His own in the world.

Jesus knows that Mary's love for Him will enable her to make the transition and embrace Him not just as "my Lord," but as the "Risen Lord." That is why He entrusts her with the command, "Go to my brethren and say to them, I am ascending to my Father and your Father, to my God and your God." In the Gospel of John, Mary Magdalene is the Apostle to the Apostles. She is the first to announce the good news of the Risen Jesus. Her great love moved Jesus to empower her to preach the Gospel message, the good news of salvation won through his suffering, death and resurrection. That is why these first days of Easter really belong to her.

If Mary Magdalene is the woman in Mark's gospel who anointed Jesus with costly aromatic nard in the house of Simon the Leper at Bethany two days before Passover, how true are his words about her: *Amen, I say you, wherever the gospel is proclaimed to the whole world, what she has done will be told in memory of her. (Mark 14:3-9).*

Mary, the husband of Joseph gave birth to Jesus in the flesh. Mary, the disciple from Magdala, gave birth to him in the Spirit. Each gave to the world a Savior; one as mother, one as Apostle. Mary, his mother, showed the body of Jesus to shepherds and kings; Mary, his apostle, having seen his risen body, can now proclaim the Risen Christ to the Church at its beginning.

A Visit To Yad Vashem

Sundown on Sunday begins the Jewish observance of Yom Shoah, Holocaust Remembrance Day. Earlier in the week, in anticipation of this day, I visited Yad Vashem, the combined Memorial and History Museum of the Holocaust in Jerusalem. Since I last visited in the year 2000, a new expanded Holocaust History Museum has been completed at the site. Situated high above the Ein Karem Valley, the beauty of the surroundings encourages thoughtful reflection and meditation. However the serenity of the site betrays the reason for being here – remembering the attempted annihilation of a people, the horrific sin of the twentieth century that was the Shoah, the Holocaust.

The natural beauty and cultivated gardens of Yad Vashem stand in stark contrast to the architecture of its buildings and monuments, which can only be described as "industrial." Concrete, steel and glass are arranged in rigid, angular patterns that remind the visitor that there is nothing soothing to be found here. The reality of what we remember is harsh and uncomfortable. The feeling conveyed is that there is always a death camp just a few steps away.

Most moving for me were the Children's Memorial and the Hall of Remembrance. The strength of both lies in their simplicity. I walked down the pathway of the Children's Memorial into a darkened, circular room. A single candle in the center of the room is reflected in hundreds of mirrors around the hall. I was surrounded by lights, appearing as stars wherever I looked. As I walked, the names of the one and one-half million Jewish children who died in the holocaust were whispered throughout the hall. There seemed to be a candle burning for each one of those children. Returning to the light of day I was confronted by a bold, larger than life sculpture of children in the arms of Father Abraham. His warm embrace welcomes to his bosom the lifeless bodies of the children being remembered. Following Jewish custom, stones are placed in memory on the memorial. The look of Abraham seems to be pondering, almost in disbelief, the promise made so long ago – a promise almost broken: *Look up at the sky and count the stars, if you can. Just so... shall your descendants be. (Genesis 15:5).*

The Hall of Remembrance is also a darkened room – large and square, with the names of the death camps inscribed on the floor; in the center of the room, an eternal flame. Like the Children's Room, this place needs no explanation. Its very silence speaks its message.

The History Museum tells the story of the Holocaust in words and pictures beginning with Hitler's rise to power and ending with the establishment of the State of Israel in 1948. Throughout the exhibition, the video testimony of survivors provides an oral history that puts names and faces to events unfolding in each of the rooms. Most unsettling for me is the question raised about the role of Pope Pius XII and the Christian Churches as the horror of the Holocaust became known to the rest of the world. History will continue to debate the question; but from my place in history, the fact that there has to be a debate at all is most disturbing.

The visit to Yad Vashem reminds me that any consideration of the Jewish world, be it political, religious or social, can only be understood in light of the Holocaust. As long as there are those who continue to deny its very existence, as long as there are those who would once again plunge the Jewish nation into the sea, the Holocaust can never be thought of only as "history." In the Museum I looked at the names on Schindler's List. Perhaps only when I look at those names and recognize one who is my father or my grandfather, my sister or my mother, will I truly understand.

Despair And Violence – Always At Our Doorstep

In these final days in Jerusalem, the sad news of the shooting at Virginia Polytechnic Institute echoes around the world. The shooting is a major story here because one of the professors who was shot, Liviu Librescu, is a Romanian Israeli and a holocaust survivor.

It is difficult to be away from home these days because I know how intensely everyone is affected when a tragedy like this happens in our own backyard. My heart is with all college students and their parents. Having worked as a campus minister at Bloomsburg University of Pennsylvania for eleven years I know that students everywhere are affected in a unique way. It is a shock for them to realize that life is not as carefree as it often appears to be during these college years.

However, it is not only college students who are deeply affected by this tragedy. Once again, we all have been made aware of our vulnerability despite our best efforts to provide for own our safety and for the security of those we love. To think that we can be free from every fear and every evil is an illusion. It is a rude awakening when we realize that our life here is not heaven. That realization is essential if we are to approach the sacredness of our lives with the reverence and respect it deserves.

Before coming to Jerusalem many friends and family members expressed concern for my safety. Their concern was well-intentioned and understandable. I had to remind them that tragedies born of violence happen within our own borders, and often with greater frequency than in some of the most troubled places in our world. It is easy to feel smug as we wonder what level of anger and despair a young Palestinian must reach that would allow him to strap explosives to his body, causing his own death and the death of countless other innocent victims. It is somewhat more sobering to realize that same level of anger and despair can happen to a lost young man living in a dorm room next to our sons and daughters one state away, or to a husband and father who barricades himself in an Amish schoolhouse in the neighboring county, killing innocent children whose heritage is one of peace and nonviolence.

While it is an obligation and necessity to provide the best of security measures for our well-being and that of our children, we delude ourselves if we think that every act of hatred and despair can be stopped by stronger locks, better metal detectors, and an arsenal of weapons. At some point we all have to come to terms with our own mortality and realize that ultimate security comes from the decision to embrace our fragile human nature and live life fully, despite the tragedies that might come our way.

Shopping At Mahane Yehuda – Preparing For Shabbat

Thus the heavens and the earth and their array were completed. Since on the seventh day God was finished with the work he had been doing, he rested on the seventh day from all the work he had undertaken. So God blessed the seventh day and made it holy, because on it he rested from all the work he had done in creation. (Genesis 2:1-3)

There is an urgency that accompanies shopping at Mahane Yehuda in the new city of Jerusalem as Shabbat approaches. Everything must be prepared and ready by sundown so the Sabbath may be observed in proper fashion. Everyday this market is alive and busy, but even more so today. I am surprised by the number of men who are shopping. Someone tells me that women are at home making final preparations and so the men take special care in choosing what food will be on the table for the Sabbath meal. For the observant Jew, each piece of fruit and every vegetable must be without stain or blemish.

The stalls are filled with every imaginable kind of food; the choices are overwhelming. The produce is fresh and inviting; dried fruits and nuts glisten in the sunlight; fish and meat are carefully prepared and packaged with pride. I almost wish I had a kitchen so I could decide – will it be fish or chicken, artichoke or rutabaga? The busiest stands seem be those with freshly baked challah and sweet rolls. Is it any wonder? The smell of the freshly baked bread and pastries fills the air. I am reminded of a saying a friend likes to repeat, "There is no such thing as gluttony when it comes to bread!" Wanting to enter into the spirit of Shabbat preparation I brave the jostling crowd and buy a small challah loaf; I am not disappointed!

The visit to Mahane Yehuda today reminds me of the Farmer's Market at home on the day before Thanksgiving. Except here in

Jerusalem the air of anticipation and feeling of excitement accompanies Shabbat preparation every week. Every Friday at sundown is reason to celebrate, reason to pray, reason to rest. For Shabbat is not simply a day free from work; it is not a day to catch up on everything you did not have the chance to do during the week; and it certainly is not the day to move from one activity to the next. It is the day to enter into rest, God's rest.

It is interesting to watch the crowd and realize that in a few short hours the hurried pace will turn to blessed rest; the candles will be lighted; the blessing said; and the Sabbath will begin. In some ways I envy the spirit of Shabbat that observant Jews have been able to maintain over the centuries, unaffected by the ways of the societies all around them; societies always in motion, never at rest.

Sabbath rest is an important theme for me because of the frantic pace at which we live our lives, and thus, by example, teach our children to live their young lives as well. We wonder why we are always tired;

we wonder why an anxious spirit has become the normal demeanor with which we approach everyday life; we wonder why it is so hard to quiet our minds and hearts to pray or even to sleep at night. The reason is simple: we make so many choices for so many good things that there is little time or energy left to choose the best thing, being at one with God and being with those whom God has given us to share our lives. That "being with at one with" is not a luxury; it is a blessing that God intended for himself and for his creation. Only all too often we convince ourselves that the world will stop spinning if we say "no" to a good thing, so that we might say "yes" to the best thing; that is, assuring our physical, emotional and spiritual well-being by quieting our minds and hearts from sundown to sundown for just one day.

This will be my last Shabbat in Jerusalem and I am going to miss it when I leave. There has been something about seeing stores closed and the streets deserted that has served as a reminder to me of the need to make a conscious effort to change my way of thinking; to stop believing that the success and well-being of my world will somehow be in danger if I take the phone off the hook, hide the car keys or let the laundry pile up for just twenty four hours! How we think about the Sabbath reflects how we think about ourselves. Do we believe that we have been made in God's image and likeness, that we are good? If so, are we willing to take the risk to follow God's lead and just for a day, rest from all that we have done?

Take care to keep holy the Sabbath day as the Lord, your God, commanded you. Six days you may labor and do all your work; but the seventh day is the Sabbath of the Lord, your God. No work may be done then, whether by you, or your son or daughter, or your male of female slave, or your ox or ass or any of your beasts, or the alien who lives with you. Your male and female slaves should rest as you do. For remember that you too were once slaves in Egypt, and the Lord, your God, brought you from there with his strong hand and outstretched arm. That is why the Lord, your God, has commanded you to observe the Sabbath day. (Deuteronomy 5: 12-15)

One More Candle And One More Falafel

This morning I went for a walk in the Old City to make one final visit to the Church of the Holy Sepulchre and say goodbye to some of the merchants I have met, who have been most gracious to me during my two month stay in Jerusalem. It might sound something of a cliché, but time has gone by very quickly and it does not seem possible that on Friday I begin a new phase of my sabbatical journey. While I feel ready to move on, walking the streets and climbing the hills this morning reminded me of how much I love the city of Jerusalem and why I wanted to be here.

I also realized that while I can describe the city and show photographs, there is no way to share the sounds and smells of Jerusalem. Whether it is the call to prayer from a minaret tower or a siren announcing a time of silence on Yom Shoah, Jerusalem is as much a feast for the ears as it is for the eyes. Today, the fragrance of saffron and cumin in the spice market and the aroma of schwarma roasting on a spit reminded that I was not at Karns or Giant!

Not surprisingly, the Church of the Holy Sepulchre was noisy and crowded with visitors so I gave up any hope of finding a prayerful corner; but I did stop to light one more candle at the tomb of Jesus and to pray for my family and friends. I also remembered those who lost their lives in the shooting at Virginia Tech this week. With the spirit of the Easter season still very much with us, I could hear the words of the angel to the women who came to the tomb: *Do not be afraid! I know that you are seeking Jesus the crucified. He is not here, for he has been raised just as he said. Come and see the place where he lay. (Matthew 28:5-6)*

I visited an art gallery in the Jewish Quarter to see Benjamin, an artist and one of the owners of the gallery. He offered me coffee and spoke at length of what it means for him to be in Jerusalem. He told me about the recent war with the Hezbollah in Lebanon and how difficult it was when there were no tourists and no one was shopping. It was difficult not only for him but for everyone who calls this place home. He said his spirit was kept alive by the many people, family, friends and clients, who called to offer him support. He thanked me for coming to Jerusalem and for appreciating the importance and significance of the city.

Of course I had to have one more falafel before leaving Jerusalem! How something as simple as chick pea paste, salad, and humus in a pita can taste so good is one of the marvels of this part of the world, right up there with the parting of the Red Sea! Maybe in my retirement I can open a schwarma and falafel stand at the Farmer's Market! I wonder, is our world ready for a little bit of Jerusalem on the West Shore?

Jerusalem – A Final Reflection

When traveling for pleasure or pilgrimage I like to ask people at the end of the day or the end of the journey to choose any particular sight they have visited or moment they have experienced that stands out as being special in some way. I have been asking myself that question the past few days as my time in Jerusalem comes to an end. I have to say there have been many times here that have had special meaning; there have been many moments of grace. From my experience I know that over time, many other moments will emerge that have had some impact on me that I might not realize now, but will in time. That is one of the graces of a pilgrimage; it continues to unfold long after the journey ends.

Since I have been here for a long time, for eight weeks, I have chosen two such moments. The first has two parts.

During the feast of Purim I walked along the Kidron Valley and stopped at an observation plaza overlooking the tombs of the prophets, the Mount of Olives, and the Garden of Gethsemane. A Jewish family arrived in holiday spirit and sat on the other side of the platform. I was marveling at the sights before me when suddenly I felt someone tapping my shoulder. I turned, and a little girl wearing a blue coat handed me a piece of candy and scurried back to her family.

Two days later I was sitting at the parvis, the entryway to the Church of the Holy Sepulchre, and a group of Arab boys were playing on the steps leading to the Christian Quarter. My guess is that they had just been dismissed from school for the day and they were very happy about it.

These two groups of children reminded me that although every stone is this land has a history, the living stones, the people of this land, also have a story to tell. It is a story about a long history of longing for peace. It is a story about peoples with a common ancestry trying to find a way to live together with an understanding and respect that is often elusive, usually beyond their reach. It is a story that makes the plea of Psalm 122 all the more urgent: *For the peace of Jerusalem pray! May those who love you prosper! May peace be within your ramparts, prosperity within your towers.*

The second experience that was a time of grace was my visit to the
Church of Saint Peter in Gallicantu soon after I arrived. The special
image that has stayed with me since that time is discovering the steps
leading from Mount Zion to the Kidron Valley, the steps that Jesus
and his disciples probably took on their way to Gethsemane after the

Last Supper.

I had read about the steps in the guidebooks and commentaries I had consulted in preparing for this trip. The reading and research on the Passion Narratives that I have been doing here in Jerusalem also mentions the steps when discussing Jesus leaving the Upper Room with his disciples. When I found them on the side of the hill next to the Church it was a blessed moment. There were no other visitors so I had time alone to read the scriptural account and pray in this special place.

All throughout the Gospels Jesus is always "on the way" somewhere; sometimes to teach, sometimes to heal, always to bring forgiveness and comfort. Descending these steps to the Kidron Valley would be his final journey before being arrested. His willingness to face his trials for the salvation of the world began here with this steep descent into a night filled with denial, betrayal, mockery and torture. *Like a lamb led to the slaughter:* he made his way, first to pray, and then to place himself into the hands of his heavenly Father; the same Father who said of him: *This is my Son, my beloved, in whom I am well pleased.*

Father Abraham also roamed these hillsides on his way to Mount Moriah to sacrifice his only son Isaac in obedience to the will of the Lord God, Yahweh. And in the end Yahweh relented and Isaac was spared. It would be God's own son, some eighteen hundred years later, who would offer the supreme sacrifice of his life for the life of the world, not on Mount Moriah, but on the Mount of Calvary.

Sitting on these steps it is hard not to think of the journey of our lives as we strive to follow the way of the Gospel. Sometimes the road is filled with Palm Sunday "Hosannas," and sometimes it is filled with cries of lament; sometimes we travel a path laden with sunlight knowing joy and fulfillment; sometimes we, like Jesus, descend into the darkness of a night filled with misunderstanding and confusion.

Yet all along the way we are guided, encouraged, and sometimes carried by the Lord Jesus who made the same journey, for there is nothing that we experience in our living that was not first experienced by Jesus himself. It is what Saint Paul meant when he wrote: *Though he was in the form of God, (Jesus) did not regard equality with God something to be grasped. Rather, he emptied himself, taking the form of a slave, coming in human likeness; and found human in appearance, he humbled himself, becoming obedient to death, even death on a cross. (Philippians 2:6-8)*

The image of the Mount Zion steps will stay with me in the days ahead as I travel to Turkey and Greece, but also long after my sabbatical pilgrimage has ended. I know that with each step I take there is grace and mercy to be had from the source of every good gift, the Lord Jesus himself. Pray for the peace of Jerusalem!

Istanbul

First Day In Istanbul – A Visit To Hagia Sophia

Yesterday I was driven to Ben Gurion Airport in Tel Aviv by an Indian Jew from Bhopal who listens to Johnny Cash. This morning I watched the sunrise over the Bosporus. Not bad for a kid from Shamokin! What a blessed opportunity I have been given in the experiences I have had in my travels during this sabbatical time!

On my first full day in Istanbul I went first, by intention, to Hagia Sophia, the sixth century church turned mosque in the 15th century, turned museum in the 20th century. In my first course in art history we studied Byzantine art and architecture. We looked at slides of San Vitale in Ravenna, San Marco in Venice, the Aachen Cathedral of Charlemagne, and Hagia Sophia. It has taken thirty years, but now I can say that I have seen each of those places in person.

Hagia Sophia means "holy wisdom." It is a masterpiece for all ages, made all the more awe-inspiring when you remember that it was built in the 6th century by the emperor Justinian. By design, its intention was to offer a view of the world that is to come. If one's spirit can not be lifted to the heavens in Hagia Sophia, it will probably not happen anyway else on earth either. The massive dome and Byzantine mosaics lead visitors to a world beyond the natural as they enter the world of the supernatural. True to the style of Byzantine art, there are no traces of nature in the decoration of the church. Rather, we are invited to leave the world of nature behind as we contemplate the mystery of God.

I was moved by the ninth century mosaic above the entrance to the church depicting the Pope Leo VI kneeling before Christ who is seated in royal majesty. The Pope's gesture of humility establishes the appropriate frame of mind for visiting the rest of the Church. We are to bow in humble adoration before the King of Heaven.

The vast expanse of Hagia Sophia draws the eye upward. Once inside the church, all attention is focused on the apse mosaic of Mary and the Child Jesus. This is not the humanistic Madonna and Child of Renaissance art; rather, this Mary and Jesus are seated in heavenly glory. In the mystery of the Incarnation, Christ may have become one like us; but we are not saved by His human nature, but rather by His divine nature. Jesus was born of a woman; but this woman was no ordinary mother. She was kept free from sin from the first moment of her conception so that her son might be free to choose the will of his heavenly Father. Mary at Hagia Sophia belongs to the world of mystery, for she conceived by the power of the Holy Spirit. Even in his infancy, this Jesus is Lord of heaven and earth.

There is another mosaic of Mary and the Child Jesus above of the side entrances of the Church. They are surrounded by the Emperors Constantine and Justinian, who present them with a model of the churches they designed. So that visitors do not miss seeing the mosaic as they leave, a mirror is strategically placed above the exit door, reflecting the mosaic that is located behind them. The optical illusion catches visitors off guard. But it is appropriate to be challenged by the image as you leave the church. For the mosaic does not belong to an historical era long past; it is contemporary in all respects as it asks present day visitors to Hagia Sophia what model of the church they present to Jesus and his Mother. It is a question every age must answer.

You Have A Friend In Istanbul

It has happened to me several times during these months of sabbatical. I turn a corner, or turn my head, and I see an old friend. It happened today at Kariye Camii. After a somewhat harrowing taxi ride around the Golden Horn I entered the Church of Saint Savior in Chora, and there, above me in the 14th century mosaics, was my good friend Joseph! What a welcomed sight for sore eyes! Because trust me, Saint Joseph is on the list of missing persons in most of Istanbul! For a long time he was even hidden at Saint Savior.

The church, as it stands today, dates to the end of the 11th century. It was restored and decorated with priceless mosaics and frescoes about 1320 after falling into disrepair after the Fourth Crusade in 1204. During Ottoman rule in 1511, it was converted into a mosque and the mosaics and frescoes were covered with plaster and paint. So Joseph and his cohort remained hidden until 1948 when the Byzantine Research Institute of Dumbarton Oaks began the cleaning and restoration of the church. At that time the church, turned mosque, was converted into a museum.

The Church was dedicated to both Jesus and Mary, so of course, their images are most prominent. Joseph appears often enough since the mosaics tell stories associated with the early life of the Blessed Mother, the betrothal of Joseph and Mary, and events in life of the Holy Family. My own particular favorite shows Joseph and Mary enrolling in the census in Bethlehem. We are accustomed to seeing images of Joseph leading Mary to Bethlehem, or to them being turned away at the inn. This scene of Joseph and Mary registering with Governor Quirinius of Syria is quite unusual. There is also a beautiful depiction, in an arch above one of the church windows, of the dream of Joseph and his leading Mary to the gates of Bethlehem for the census.

Many of the stories pictured in the mosaics come from the apocryphal Gospel of Saint James, a book that is not part of the New Testament. The four canonical gospels reveal very little about the lives of Joseph and Mary apart from the few passages in the infancy narratives of Matthew and Luke. Throughout the centuries, the apocryphal gospels have often been referenced to provide additional information for "curious minds!" I think this is an interesting point for consideration.

Although the style of the mosaics at Saint Savior in Chora is decidedly Byzantine, they are significantly different from the 6th century mosaics at Hagia Sophia and others from that same time period. I wrote about those images in the entry entitled "First Day in Istanbul at Hagia Sophia." Those mosaics are classic Byzantine – the figures are hieratic, that is they attempt to portray things divine, reality beyond the natural order. But at Saint Savior there is a change. The figures of Jesus, Mary, Joseph and the other saints are beginning to appear three dimensional, they have volume; they are real bodies in real space. Unlike earlier Byzantine mosaics, these figures are often seen in profile, in movement. They have personalities, unlike the earlier figures whose full frontal stares offer no clue as to what they are thinking or feeling. Their purpose is to lead you beyond the natural to the supernatural. On the contrary, the Chora figures invite you consider the human implications of the mysteries being represented. What was Joseph thinking? How did Mary feel? There is a charming scene that could be taken from any contemporary baby photo album – it shows Mary, guided by her nursemaid, taking her first seven steps toward Saint Anne. To provide a feeling of movement, the nurse's cape billows in the breeze. Those seven steps of the child Mary are a giant leap forward! Both the style and subject matter of the mosaics move humanistic concerns to the forefront, not only in the world of art, but also in the world of theology and spirituality.

It is significant that these images in Istanbul were made at the same time Giotto was painting in Padua and Assisi. Just as his paintings began to reflect the humanistic ideals of the early Renaissance, so, too, the mosaic artists of Saint Savior in Chora led the Byzantine world to a natural rendering the art world of the east had not seen since the time of classical Greece and Rome. What led to the dramatic shift? After centuries of an established style of art reflecting a theology emphasizing the power and grandeur of God, why was there a change? Why did the once haloed saints and ethereal angels begin to look like you and me?

At the risk of oversimplifying, the answer lies with one man known as "il poverello" – Francis of Assisi. With Francis' Canticle of the Creatures, the heavenly bodies, once thought to be beyond our reach, are now called Brother Sun, and Sister Moon. For the first time in a thousand years, in Giotto's paintings people look at one another. It all happened because, faithful to the gospel teaching of Jesus, Francis taught us to look at one another as brothers and sisters. With Francis, we no longer have to be afraid of our humanity; we celebrate it. Our humanity was the vehicle Jesus used to reach out to us. For centuries, the world of theology and spirituality placed Jesus and the saints in the heavens so far above us that they were beyond our reach. Francis tells us not to soar to the heavens to escape from our humanity; he teaches us to embrace it as we walk the earth, heads held high with the dignity that is ours as children of God. It is interesting to note that at the time the church thought the mysteries of heaven were too sublime for our sinful natures to comprehend, popular piety turned to Mary. If we were not worthy to approach Jesus, at least we could talk with His mother! That piety was responsible for the construction of the great Gothic cathedrals throughout Europe, most of which are dedicated to Mary.

It seems that at those times when theology and church practice spotlighted human weakness, often leaving God's amazing grace in the shadows, the piety of the faithful called us back to a spiritual balance. It is what we call "sensus fidelium" – the sensitivity and sensibility of the faithful. Echoing Saint Paul, Francis of Assisi reminded the church that, in Christ, our humanity was changed; in Christ the old order had passed away; in Christ we became a new creation. The Mosaics in the Chora Church begin to give witness to this teaching, which is at the heart of the New Testament message.

Perhaps that is why I find Joseph such an appealing figure and look for him everywhere, even in Istanbul! His gentle humanity, in the face of great mystery, reminds me that I am invited to become a part of the mystery of God, *as I am*. I do not have to pose for God. I do not have to wear a halo. I do not have to pretend to be out of this world. In fact, the more I am in touch with what is good and true and beautiful in my humanity, the more likely it is that I will hear God's voice in the gentle breeze of a spring day, or see His face in the smiles and tears of those who walk the earth just as I do, one foot in front of the other, one step at a time. I may stumble at times, but never falter; smiling all along the way at the cartoons we make just by being alive.

Get Thee To A Bath

Well, who could resist? My guidebook assured me that no trip to Istanbul would be complete without a visit to a Turkish Bath, after which my whole body would feel rejuvenated! So, why not? After all, the very modern, state of the art fitness center of the hotel where I am staying has its own bath (hamam). I would not even have to leave the front door to participate in a social, cultural ritual as old as Istanbul itself. Realizing that there is more to the city to experience than the ancient Byzantine mosaics that have been the centerpiece of my touring, I decided it was time to take the plunge and find out what the hoopla was all about. I mean, who could resist the promise of a whole body feeling rejuvenated? So one afternoon, after a delightful lunch at the Spice Market and probably too many cups of Turkish coffee, in a caffeinated frenzy I determined the time had come. Let me tell you how it is done.

First, let it be said that I chose the hours reserved for men only. One new cultural ritual at a time is about all my western psyche can handle. I knew I was not ready for a co-ed bathing experience, even though modesty is assured for all bathers. In the locker room you wrap yourself in a pestemal (best described as a dish towel on steroids) and don a pair of slippers for walking on the hot, wet marble floor.

The focal room of the experience is the bararet, or hot room. Octagonal in shape and beautifully decorated with Turkish tiles, the room is toasty warm with an array of ornate marble basins. I had the advantage of arriving at the bararet at the same time as a gentleman who seemed to know the routine, so I simply followed his lead. Begin by selecting a basin and fill it with water to the temperature of your liking. Then, using a silver bowl (that would make a handsome planter), douse yourself in water and smile serenely, as though sitting in a wet

191

dish towel is what you have been longing to do for weeks. Then the real fun begins.

Bathers, start scrubbing! A small bar of soap and course mitt is provided to help you with the "exfoliating" body scrub. Exfoliate is my new word for the day. Evidently it is very big in this part of the world. To give you an idea of how the experience is feeling about now, go into the back yard, sit in the tool shed, turn the garden hose on yourself and start rubbing your back with a rake. It seems the rejuvenation part has not taken effect yet. It should be noted that it is possible to pay someone to do the scrubbing for you. The fitness center brochure calls this service, "kese." It costs 115 New Turkish Lire. I decided not to take advantage of this luxury. After all, there is only so much a clergy renewal grant is willing to pay for!

After the scrubbing you make you way to the steam room, where you are invited "to sit and sweat for as long as you like." Now how do you know how much sweating is to your liking? Since the brochure did not offer any insights, I decided that about the time I was feeling I needed another bath was long enough. Back to the bararet! More scrubbing, more rinsing. Is there room enough in my suitcase for one of these silver bowls? I saw them in the Old Bazaar but had no idea they had such cultural significance.

By this time additional bathers were walking from the camekan (entrance hall) to the bararet (who thinks up these names?) and one Japanese visitor seems to have opted for a "pummeling full-body massage." This means that he is lying on what looks like a marble coffee table (gobek tasi) while one of the attendants, also clad in a dish towel, is doing the pummeling. If you are still trying to experience this vicariously, at this point invite someone to join you in the back yard and have him pinch your back repeatedly and rhythmically while you are draped over a lighted gas grill.

It seemed to me that my rejuvenation experience had come to an end. For those who had opted for one of the paid services, hot apple tea was awaiting them in the camekan as they left. For the rest of us, heavily lemoned iced-water was provided. Until this moment I have been careful to document my travel experiences with numerous photographs. However, I did not think it would be acceptable to Turkish sensibilities to enter the baraet, clad in my pestemal, with camera in hand! So you will have to use your imagination to visualize my attempt at full-body rejuvenation!

The Silent Stones Speak

To walk the corridors of the Archeological Museum in Istanbul is to visit the civilizations of the many peoples who thrived in this part of the world throughout the centuries. A pair of Hittite portal lions from sixth century B.C. greets visitors at the gate and prepares them for the experience. Although the collection was begun only in the 19th century, governors ruling in the provinces of the Ottoman Empire sent artifacts to Istanbul from many distant lands. I went to the museum specifically to see one ancient stone; but was overwhelmed by the riches to be found in the entire collection and spent several hours marveling at the artistic mastery of civilizations dating back to the 13th century B.C.

I learned about the stone that prompted my visit here while preparing for my stay in Jerusalem. The story is told in the second book of Chronicles, chapter 32. In the 7th century B.C. Hezekiah, King of Judah, prepared the city for an impending attack by Sennacherib, the king of Assyria. Sennacherib had already conquered the Kingdom of Israel in the north. Hezekiah cut a 533 meter tunnel in the rock to redirect the water supply flowing from the Gihon spring, the only source of water for the city. He directed the water to flow into a pool that was located within the city walls. In that way the residents living within the walls would have a supply of water during the attack. The pool is called the Siloam and both the tunnel and the pool still function today. At the southern end of the tunnel, where the water reaches the pool, an inscription in Hebrew carved in limestone told the story of the building of the canal. The stone was discovered in 1880 and taken to Istanbul in 1882.

Recall Gospel story that telling us that Jesus cured a blind man by spitting on the ground and making clay, which he then put on the man's eyes. Jesus told him to go and wash in the pool of Siloam. The man obeyed, and he was healed (John 9:1-41). The miracle led to a great controversy between Jesus and the Pharisees because it happened on the Sabbath.

The stone in the Istanbul Archeological Museum fills in the missing archeological piece of Hezekiah's puzzle and completes the story. I marvel at the way archeologists, historians and scripture scholars are able to weave together bits of evidence to provide a clearer picture of what is happening in the Bible stories that are so familiar. The more we are able to use all of the tools of scholarship in our study of the Word of God, the more that Word will speak to us of the mystery of God's wisdom. In the case of the waters of the Gihon spring flowing into the Pool of Siloam, it is a story of the mystery of God's saving power revealed both in the Old and New Testament. Jesus will bring that saving power to its fulfillment, for as he tells the Samaritan woman at the well: *Whoever drinks of the water that I shall give will never thirst; the water that I shall give will become in him a spring of water welling up to eternal life (John 4:14).*

Final Thoughts On Leaving Istanbul

For the next phase of my travels I have joined a small group of tourists for two final days of touring in Istanbul and a cruise to Ephesus, Patmos and several of the Greek Islands. I look forward to visiting those places important in the missionary journeys of Saint Paul, and to visiting the cave in Patmos where Saint John wrote the Book of Revelation. In Ephesus I will have the opportunity to visit the chapel built over the house where tradition says Saint John cared for the Blessed Mother during her final days on earth. As I did when leaving Rome and Jerusalem I have been asking myself if there have been any special experiences or moments during the days in Istanbul that have had special meaning for me, or that have provided an opportunity for new insights or for continued reflection.

After a long day of touring in the city I had the opportunity to speak with our guide while we waited for others in the group to assemble. We talked for some time about the current political situation in Turkey as members of Parliament try to select a new president. His insights helped me to understand the process as well as the complexities and difficulties facing Turkey, a nation with a secular government but whose people are almost exclusively followers of Islam. He then told me a little about his own life situation.

He was born in Turkey but is an Armenian Orthodox Christian. His three year old twin daughters were born in the United States and were baptized in the Armenian cathedral in Jerusalem. He told me that it is very difficult to live as a member of the Christian minority in Turkey. Throughout his life he learned what he needs to do to get by. However, he and his wife do not think that their daughters should have to face the same trials. They plan to move to the United States before their children start school where they will be a part of a strong

Armenian community who share their faith and values.

His story reminded me of the Christian minority in the Holy Land who also find it increasingly difficult to remain in a place where the future is so uncertain. In a nation where they are in the minority, Christians in Israel face constant political and religious struggles, including oppression, from those who are in the majority.

The plight of the Christians living in Turkey reminds me of the mosaics in Hagia Sophia. When the church became a mosque, historic Christian mosaics were covered with plaster and paint. Now that it is a museum, attempts are being made to remove the plaster but the process of uncovering the images is quite difficult. Because of their age and delicate condition, some of the images will have to wait to be uncovered until a new technique can be learned. It will take some time for the face of Christ to emerge.

My time in this part of the world has reminded me that the freedom of religion that we, in America, cherish and work so hard to protect in America is a right not to be taken lightly. It was no accident that an American intervention at the Second Vatican Council brought about the Document of Religious Freedom, a milestone in the emerging understanding of our Church on the importance of ensuring and respecting individual faith expression and freedom of conscience. Because American Catholics have faced prejudice and discrimination throughout the history of our nation perhaps we understand, better than most, the importance of religious freedom for all people.

It is a lesson that has important implications for our present day as we wrestle with questions about immigration and how to treat those who have come to our land seeking the same freedom and the same opportunity our ancestors assured for us not so many years ago. My time in Israel and in Turkey has convinced me that we, as a Church and as American Catholics, have an important leadership role to play as our nation seeks to find ways to ensure our security and ways to treat those who seek to regularize their status in a nation which boasts to being "the home of the free." We need to be a voice for those who are sincerely asking for that which has been given to us by virtue of our place of birth. I fear that if we simply close our borders, without finding a way to open our hearts to share what belongs to all of God's children, we are little better than those abroad who deny others the right to live and to worship freely. The freedom we know in America belongs to us not by virtue of our citizenship; it belongs to us by virtue of our humanity. Freedom is not a possession we dole out to those we deem to be worthy; it is a right belonging to all of God's children who share our planet. If we are quick to deny that freedom to those who seek it, we become the ones doing the plastering and painting, covering up the face of the compassionate Christ that so needs to be revealed in a world too often enamored by its own reflection.

Onto to Greece, the birthplace of democracy and the land where Saint Paul preached his most memorable sermons.

Sailing the Aegean

Taking Mary Into Our Hearts

On the top of a mountain, beyond the borders of the ancient city of Ephesus, a small chapel captures the spiritual imagination of pilgrims who come to visit what is called "The House of the Virgin Mary." An ancient tradition says that Mary spent her final days in Ephesus in the home of the Apostle John. The words of the Fourth Gospel come to mind: *Standing by the cross of Jesus were his mother, and his mother's sister, Mary the wife of Cleopas, and Mary Magdalene. When Jesus saw his mother and the disciple there whom he loved, he said to his mother, "Woman, behold, your son." Then he said to the disciple, "Behold your mother." And from that hour the disciple took her into his home. (John 19:25-27)*

Like many of the ancient traditions of our faith, we may never be able to confirm, with certainty, whether Mary actually lived with the Beloved Disciple on a remote mountain in Turkey. What draws people to the sight is an appreciation of what is being remembered here – the loving relationship of John and the Blessed Mother. That relationship is a metaphor for the relationship the entire church has with Mary. It is as though, in speaking to the Beloved Disciple from the Cross, Jesus was addressing believers of every age, inviting them to a relationship of love and spiritual affection with His mother.

The "House of the Virgin Mary" is a small chapel built on first century ruins. It is a place of quiet prayer for all who visit. Nearby people drink blessed water from an ancient spring and leave scarves and other mementos on a prayer wall, seeking Mary's intercession. I was not aware of this tradition before visiting the sight but another person in our tour group was. She was gracious in giving me a small grey scarf that she had made. I placed it on the wall as I prayed for those people and for those intentions that are close to my heart. This simple gesture reminded me of the story of Saint Paul when he was in Ephesus. The Acts of the Apostles (19:11-12) tells us: *So extraordinary were the mighty deeds God accomplished at the hands of Paul that when face cloths or aprons that touched his skin were applied to the sick, their diseases left then and the evil spirits came out of them.*

We entrust our joys and sorrows, our hopes and our fears to those who are closest to us in life. Perhaps that is the nature of intercessory prayer. We entrust our hearts to those saints whose lives resonate with our own. Here pilgrims entrust their prayers to Mary as they would share themselves with family and friends. In this place of prayer we respond to the words of Jesus on the cross; seeking Mary's intercession is how we take her into our hearts as we share with her our deepest longings.

It is interesting that followers of Islam also revere this sight. Mary is one of the few women mentioned in the Koran. On August 15th, the feast of the Assumption of Mary, followers of the prophet Mohammed visit and pray at this shrine. Perhaps it will Mary's intercession that will bring an end to the misunderstanding and violence that is tearing apart families and nations, all in the name of God (Allah).

Whenever we speak the name of Mary it is with great reverence and respect. That reverence and respect is very much in evidence for all who come to this out of the way place, on a mountain in western Turkey, to pray and to honor the woman we call our spiritual mother. Our prayer to her is how we, like the beloved disciple, take her into our hearts.

Reading John On The Island
Of Patmos

*I, John, your brother, who share with you the distress, the kingdom,
and the endurance we have in Jesus, found myself on the island called
Patmos because I proclaimed God's word and gave testimony to Jesus. I
was caught up in the spirit on the Lord's day and heard behind me a voice
as loud as a trumpet, which said: "Write on a scroll what you see and send
it to the seven churches: to Ephesus, Smyrna, Pergamum, Thyatira, Sardis,
Philadelphia, and Laodicea." (Revelation 1"9-11)*

Patmos is smaller in size and population than many of the other
isles in the Dodecanese, but its importance in the world of the Christian
faith gives it a stature that is second to none in the island chain of
the Aegean Sea. For it was here that an angel was sent to John the
Theologian with a revelation that he was commanded to write down
for the seven churches of Asia Minor, that they might persevere in faith
during a time of trial and tribulation.

John received his vision in a cave that lies above the harbor town
of Skala and beneath Chora, the highest point on the island and site
of the 12th century Monastery of Saint John. Truly, this is one of the
most sacred mountains in the universe of faith. Its historical value was
testified to by the United Nations Educational, Scientific and Cultural
Organization which named it to the "List of World Heritage Sights,"
assuring that it would "be protected for the benefit of all humanity."

I visited the Cave of the Apocalypse early one morning and witnessed
the power of the site that affects even the most skeptical of visitors. I
have been moved many times and in many places while traveling these
past four months, but the experience here in the cave was somehow
different. The words that best describe what I felt are "quiet intensity"
and "felt presence." Upon later reflection I realized that those words

also describe the way I feel when I read the Book of Revelation. The intense beauty of the place surely influenced the richness of expression found in the book John wrote here; and, in turn, the expressive tone of John's writing is reflected in the geography of the place where the book was written. Throughout the centuries there continues to be a spiritual give and take between sacred space and sacred writing: the place inspired the book, and, in turn, the book continues to give life to this most holy place and all who visit here.

Tradition tells us that when John was exiled here in 90 A.D. he dictated his revelations to the scribe Prochorus. A large mosaic above the entrance to the Monastery records the event and establishes the tone for the visit to the cave. The mosaic tells visitors that something sacred happened here, something beyond the ordinary character of everyday life. The hand of the scribe may have written the text, but it was the mouth of God that spoke the words he wrote – words repeated by his human instrument, the theologian John. When I visited the cave a young student from the nearby Patmias School was being instructed in the singing of Orthodox liturgical chant. His chanting added to the solemnity of the visit.

The Book of Revelation is probably the most misunderstood book of the New Testament. Many use it as a kind of crystal ball, trying to see the future in the visions that John shares with his readers. But John was not predicting the future as much as he was telling the story of the past. True to the nature of apocalyptic literature, he used exaggerated, symbolic language to tell stories of the past; but he tells those stories using the future tense. The style of writing and literary form may seem strange to us in our day, but it followed in the same tradition as some of the later Old Testament books, like the prophet Daniel.

John wrote during a time of intense persecution for the infant church. In the beginning verses he tells his readers that he shares their faith in Jesus and also in their tribulation. To offer them encouragement in their suffering John urges them to live with the "patient endurance" that has been the trademark of people of faith throughout the ages. Just as God has triumphed in the lives of people who remained steadfast in past generations, so too in the present age God will again make his dwelling with his beloved. What encouraging words John offers to us when he writes: *He will wipe away every tear from their eyes, and there shall be no more death or mourning, wailing or pain, for the old order has passed away. (Revelation 21:4).*

When I read the Book of Revelation I am reminded of the disciples, after the Ascension, when they were asked by the angels why they were standing looking up to the heavens. The visions of John are not to be seen as some kind of spiritual jigsaw puzzle nor are they to be treated as a mystical treasure hunt. Rather, those visions reach back to the past and give meaning for the present age. To see the Book of Revelation as a telling of the future is to rob it of its power to strengthen us in the present day living of the Gospel message when faced with challenge and uncertainty. Reading the assuring words of John, the Theologian, fill the believer with the quiet intensity and felt presence of Jesus that I experienced on an early morning in the Cave at Patmos.

And I heard a loud voice from the throne saying, "Behold, God's dwelling is with the human race. He will dwell with them and they will be his people and God himself will always be with them. (Revelation 21:3).

With Paul In Ephesus

The ancient Roman city of Ephesus, in western Turkey, was home to 200,000 people. The ruins of the city attract tens of thousands of visitors every year. The façade of the Library of Celsus, built in 114 A.D., is one of the most recognizable images of the ancient world and probably the most photographed place among the ruins. However it is another sight in Ephesus that also commands attention. It is the ancient road that led to the port of Ephesus. Many people recognize it as the road that Anthony and Cleopatra walked when they came to Ephesus, after proclaiming themselves husband and wife. As interesting as that might be, I found myself staring in awe because this is the road that Saint Paul must have used when he came to Ephesus during his third missionary journey.

Paul spent considerable time preaching in Ephesus. His letter to the believers of this city is filled with praise for their steadfast faith and for their "love toward all the saints." After preaching in the synagogue, during his time here, he found many believers, but also encountered much opposition when he tried when he tried to preach in the great theatre on the side of Mount Pion.

The reason for the opposition is quite interesting, as described in chapter 19 in the Acts of the Apostles. Paul's opposition came from the silversmith Demetrius. The reason for his opposition was not theological, but rather financial. As a silversmith, Demetrius made his living carving votive statues for the shrine of Artemis. Paul's preaching the good news of the one true God was a threat to Demetrius' livelihood. So he gathered together other silver and goldsmiths and convinced them that Paul was a threat.

He said: *Men, you know well that our prosperity derives from this work. As you can now see and hear, not only in Ephesus but throughout*

most of the province of Asia this Paul has persuaded and misled a great
number of people by saying that gods made by hands are not gods at all.
The danger grows, not only that our business will be discredited, but also
that the temple of the great god Artemis will be of no account, and that she
whom the whole province of Asia and all the world worship will be stripped
of her magnificence. (Acts 19:25-27)

As a result of Demetrius' action some of Paul's disciples, fearing for his safety, kept him from entering the theatre to preach. With that, Paul left Ephesus and set sail for Macedonia. Perhaps that is why he would later write these words of reminder to the faithful of the city: *For we are his handiwork, created in Christ Jesus for the good works that God has prepared in advance, that we should live in them. (Ephesians 2:10)* With his preaching Paul turned the tables on Demetrius. We do not to fashion God in our image, according to our imaginings, as did Demetrius and the other silversmiths of the Artemis cult. Rather, we are *God's* handiwork, formed in *His* image and likeness.

Like all of the stories in the scriptures, Paul's experience in Ephesus challenges me in my life of faith. In what do I find my security? In what do I place my trust? Do I conclude that it is the work of my hands that provides for my well-being; am I a modern day Demetrius? Or rather do I recognize that I am God's handiwork and that my happiness will be found in the good works that my faith bids me do? Paul may not have been able to preach in the great theatre of Ephesus, but his words continue to instruct, to encourage and to challenge. Walking the road that Paul himself traveled brings that preaching to new life and new light for this follower of the way.

Athens

Remember Who You Are

In the movie *Yentyl*, after disguising herself as a boy and learning that she has been accepted into a yeshiva to study the Talmud, Barbra Streisand sings: "There are moments you remember for the rest of your life... this is one of those moments." Those were my sentiments when I passed through the Propylea (gate) of the Acropolis and saw before me the Erechtheion and the Parthenon. I had studied and taught these ancient temples in art history classes. Now the buildings I had known as photographs in a book were present before me, and I was mesmerized. I remember having a similar experience when I first saw Michelangelo's Roman *Pieta* at the New York World's Fair in 1964. What belonged to a time long ago and a land far away was suddenly within my reach. Standing on the Acropolis on a sunny morning in May, it was as if all that I had imagined about ancient Greece was now at my doorstep.

The word "acropolis" means "upper city." Although it is not the highest hill in Athens, the Acropolis commands the most attention and respect. Turn a corner anywhere in the center of the city and look up and you may be treated to a view of the Parthenon, the Propylea, the Erechteion or the Temple of Athena Nike. Hotels and restaurants boast "acropolis views" in their advertising, and sitting in a small taverna beneath the "upper city" seems to be on the "to do" list of most visitors.

The Acropolis was developed in the fifth century B.C. during the Golden Age of Pericles. It was designed to serve as the religious center of the city in celebration of the victory of the Greeks over the Persians. Pericles employed the finest architects and sculptors to honor the gods as well as reflect the dignity and grace of the human spirit, hallmarks of the Greek view of humanity.

Our guide for the tour of the Acropolis was a very knowledgeable young woman who spoke with passion about the significance of the sight. I could not help but think of her as the Melina Mercouri of the archeological world! When the tour ended I had an opportunity to ask her about the possibility of the Parthenon sculptures being returned to Greece from the British Museum. "It will never happen," she said. "We are building a new museum for them but we will never see them. There are over one million Greek artifacts in museums all over the world, and still we have the only national archeological museum in the world that only displays items from its own country. I went to Copenhagen to lecture last year and visited their museum to see something different. It was filled with things from the classical Greek world! We are everywhere," she said laughing.

When I told her that I had been waiting for forty years to see the Acropolis she nodded with understanding. "Of course I am proud of this place because I am Greek," she told me. "And I still appreciate it as a religious sight. Do not misunderstand, I do not believe in the gods of the ancient world. I am a Christian. But these gods are a part of our history. They are a part of who we were then. And in every society, who we were then determines who we are now."

Two days later, while sitting in an Athens Starbucks (I could not resist!) and thinking about her words, I suddenly realized why I had such a felt reaction while visiting the Acropolis and the Agora (the ancient marketplace) the next day. The buildings and ruins of ancient Greece resonate with me not only because I have studied them. They are also a part of my history; they play a role in how I understand myself. The art, architecture, religion, literature, language, and law of the western world have their roots in ancient Greece. Socrates, Plato, Aristotle, Homer, Solon and Aristophanes are our ancestors. We may be not be born of Greek ancestry, but Greek ideals are in our psychological and spiritual DNA. Those ideals influence how we think and how we reason. I am reminded of the comic scenes in "My Big Fat Greek Wedding" when the father of the bride goes to great lengths to explain how every English word comes from the Greek language! Even though exaggerated, there is wisdom in his words.

Today I paid a second visit to the Archeological Museum along with several groups of school children there on a field trip. Seeing them seated on the floor around an ancient Greek statue, while listening to the explanation of their teachers, made me think of how important it is to know where we come from. These children have a direct connection to the objects they were seeing, yet all of us have intellectual, political and spiritual ties to the Greek world. I think that is why I treasure the liberal arts education I received throughout my schooling. I still believe that a strong foundation in literature, language, history and the arts is the best preparation for life, no matter the profession to which we aspire. If we know how to think, how to reason, and how to express ourselves we have all the foundation we need for a meaningful life.

I used to encourage my art history students not to sell their textbook at the end of the semester. I told them that in future years they would find that, at day's end, their spirits would need to be nourished. Being reminded of the beauty that is a part of our western heritage does more to revive our spirits than any passing fad or instant gratification.

As a young boy I remember my mother telling me when I left the house, "Remember who you are." Her words still hold sway throughout these past four months as I have been visiting my spiritual roots in Rome, Jerusalem, and now in Athens. I have had many blessed opportunities in the places I have seen to remember who I am, because I have been able to see where I have come from.

Paul Speaks To The Athenians – Paul Speaks To Us

While Paul was waiting for them at Athens, he grew exasperated at the sight of the city full of idols… Then Paul stood up at the Areopagus and said: "You Athenians, I see that in every respect you are very religious. For as I walked around looking carefully at your shrines, I even discovered an altar inscribed, 'To an Unknown God.' What therefore you unknowingly worship, I proclaim to you… (Acts of the Apostles 17, passim)

It should come as no surprise that Saint Paul preached in Athens. Looking at a map of his missionary journeys, he seems to have preached everywhere in the Mediterranean world. However, for Paul Athens was not just another stop along the way for the Apostle to the Gentiles. He knew that the city had special significance in the religious world of the time and as a result his preaching there took on a more urgent tone.

At the time of Paul's preaching, Athens and the other Greek city states had been under the control of the Roman Empire from the middle of the second century B.C. as part of the province called Macedonia. During this time the Greeks were permitted to maintain their own language and cultural identity. When it came to religion, Rome actually adopted many of the religious ways of the Greeks and made them their own. Zeus became Jupiter, Athena became Minerva. So when Paul went to Athens he was going to where pagan religion, as it was being practiced throughout much of the Roman empire, had its beginnings.

As was his custom, Paul first sought out the devout members of the synagogue in Athens and preached the Gospel to them. He then moved into the market place, the Agora, and following the tradition of Socrates, Plato and Aristotle, he entered into argument with the Epicurean and Stoic philosophers of the day. Puzzled by Paul's preaching about Jesus and the resurrection of the dead they took him to the Areopagus, a hill beneath the Acropolis that served as the location of the courts and the place where judgments were rendered. It was here, within the hearing of the priests of the Acropolis temples, that Paul preached his best known sermon.

Paul's preaching was respectful in tone. He began by acknowledging the strong religious tradition of the citizens of Athens, but in usual Pauline style, his preaching was also direct and to the point. God cannot be defined by human inventions and imaginings, for God himself *gives to everyone life and breath and everything.* Paul tells the Areopagites that the Creator *has fixed the ordered seasons and the boundaries of their regions, so that people might seek God, even perhaps grope for him and find him.* It was a theme Paul would later to develop in his letter to the Romans: *We know that all creation is groaning in labor pains even until now; and not only that, but we ourselves, who have the first fruits of the Spirit, we also groan within ourselves as we wait for adoption, the redemption of our bodies. (Romans 8:22-24)*

It was bold of Paul to preach so strong a message in so significant a place. He challenged the very principles of the pagan world, whose religion tried to control or domesticate the gods by the fashioning and worshipping of idols. Paul told the citizens of Athens: *Since therefore we are the offspring of God, we ought not to think that the divinity is like an image fashioned from gold, silver, or stone by human art and imagination. (Acts 17:29).* Followers of "the way" see things differently. True religion seeks not to control but to serve the Spirit of God that is within each person. God *is not far from any one of us,* Paul said. *In him we live and move and have our being,* he continued, quoting the Greek poets.

On the day I visited the Acropolis it was moving for me to see the guide point below us and say, "There is the Areopagus." I was moved not only because I was seeing the actual hill where Paul preached, but also because the message he preached on that hill is one that I often return to in my own thinking and preaching.

Religion is not a system of belief that is imposed on us. There is, rather, a spark of the divine within each of us, what we call the indwelling of the Holy Spirit. We listen attentively to that voice within and discern how and where we are being lead in life by the Spirit of God. Religion, the belief system we embrace and the rituals we follow, flow from that discernment. The structure of our life of faith (our particular religion) is intended to provide external support to the movement of the spirit within. Communal sharing of the action of the Holy Spirit within each of us provides direction and discernment for the life of faith we share with others. Religion is at its best when it encourages and frees a person to live a spirit-filled life. Religion loses its integrity when it instills fear or when it imposes a way of life or preaches a view of the human person that is not consonant with the voice within, speaking to the heart and soul of a person.

Again, in his letter to the Romans Paul explains: *For those who are led by the Spirit of God are children of God. For you did not receive a spirit of slavery to fall back into fear, but you received a spirit of adoption, through which we cry "Abba, Father!" The Spirit itself bears witness with our spirit that we are children of God... (Romans 8:14-16).*

On the Areopagus Paul dared the Athenians to place their trust not in objects made of gold and silver, but in the Holy Spirit dwelling within each person. That Holy Spirit is the gift Jesus promised to his disciples, a promise he was able to fulfill only when he was raised from the dead. Perhaps that is why the Athenians struggled with the idea of the resurrection – it challenged the very foundation of their thinking and practice of religion. It invited them to put their hope not in objects they could hold in their hands, in the externals of religion, but in the Risen One they could know only by faith when they listened to the voice within. As Paul told the Church of Rome: *For in hope we were saved. Now hope that sees for itself is not hope. For who hopes for what one sees? But is we hope for what we do not see, we wait with endurance. (Romans 8:24-25)*

Hyacinths To Feed The Soul

The Plaka district of Athens winds its way north and east around the foot of the Acropolis. Its shops, restaurants and cafes attract tourists and locals alike. The area is pedestrian friendly and the mood is festive. The other day I spent several hours walking in the Plaka, enjoying the architecture and the spirit of the place. I turned a corner and caught sight of a shop displaying carpets and textiles and realized that I had not provided an update on my "carpet experiences" during these past few weeks of travel in Turkey and Greece. Yes, that is "experiences" in the plural. I am beginning to think that along with the indelible mark embedded on my soul at baptism, a sign visible only to rug merchants reading "try to sell this man a carpet" was placed above my head as well!

It started in the Old City of Jerusalem and continued in Istanbul. At the Arasta Bazaar I had lunch in a lovely outdoor café in the shadows of the Blue Mosque. I then walked past a shop displaying beautiful carpets and you know what happened next. Within minutes I was in the shop sipping apple tea. However, this was no folding chair welcome like the souk in Old City Jerusalem. With this store I had reached the nirvana of rugdom. Uti was my host and he insisted that I sit on a lovely couch covered with Turkish killams. I was starting to feel like Ali Baba; the aroma of the apple tea and the beauty the rugs were intoxicating. I wondered if perhaps merchants slip a potion in the tea they offer that sends a message to the brain saying "You need to spend lots of money in a hurry!" In this shop there were no high pressure tactics. The approach was more subtle, and I suspect that a welcoming spirit and graceful manner are more convincing than a magic potion in the apple tea.

Uti began by asking me what type of carpet I found beautiful.

"Small," I blurted out! He knew that meant "cheap!" So he ordered his assistant to bring out several small pieces that I might "find interesting." His assistant smiled and affirmed every word Uti uttered. He was a kind of Ed McMahon to Uti's Johnny Carson-like commanding presence.

Of course, the carpets selected for my viewing were beautiful. Several, that were within my price range, caught my attention and I was sure that if I expressed an interest in any of them, Uti would be making a better offer than the listed price. I never had the chance, because Uti asked permission to show me one more carpet that had arrived just last week. I knew I was once again in over my head as Ed McMahon collected all of the "small" carpets and put them out of sight. He then unrolled the most beautiful carpet I have ever seen – an area rug of deep blues, reds and greens showing every genus and specie of flora and fauna imaginable. Uti offered no explanation of the carpet; he simply said, "We are going to leave you alone for awhile." Then he and Ed left the store!

I knew exactly what was happening. I have read those stories about newly-hatched baby ducklings that attach themselves to the first moving thing they encounter. Uti and Ed were counting on that kind of bonding experience taking place during my time alone with this Hereke beauty. I sat and looked at the carpet for awhile and then walked around to see it from different angles and in a different light. I am afraid the bonding was beginning to happen. After ten minutes Uti knocked on the door of his own shop and asked if I was in a hurry. "In a hurry? I am sitting in the middle of old town Istanbul, seven time zones away from home. What else do I have to do today?" I invited Uti and Ed to return to their own store!

Then something happened that made me nervous. Uti said that he wanted to show me "something very special" and turned off all the lights! What is the Turkish phrase for "I need to leave immediately?" He and Ed held the carpet against the glass door so that I could see the "quality of the workmanship and brilliance of the colors in the natural light of the sun." I was beginning to wonder if I would have to hang the carpet in my front window to fully appreciate its beauty!

The lights came back on and Uti showed me a map in what seemed to be a carpet bible so that I would know exactly where in Turkey my new duckling had been hatched. We then spoke about price, better yet "prices" if I wanted to include one of the "smaller" carpets in the purchase since it adds just "a few more dollars to the cost" of shipping! I explained to Uti that a carpet was an investment and I would never make such an important decision on the spur of the moment. He liked the part about a carpet being an investment! He was very respectful of my decision to take time to think about this purchase. Early on he had asked me how long I would be staying in Istanbul so he knew he had me for five more days. These guys do not miss anything! He also told me that he was sure he could offer a better price once I had decided to buy this carpet, which "obviously means so much to you!" And with that we parted good friends!

I did consider buying the carpet but was still not certain the bonding experience had been the real thing or if the potion-laden tea had taken its effect. So I left Istanbul without a carpet. Not to worry though, there would be many more opportunities. Like the "the unique opportunity to shop in a quality establishment" in Kusadasi provided by the tour guide at the end of the visit to Ephesus! Or perhaps I should say the "commissioned" tour guide!

This "quality establishment" was quite the place – upscale, sleek, Tiffany-like in appearance with sales personnel draped in gold and dressed to the nines. There was no apple tea here. This was a wine and special Turkish snacks kind of place. The experience began with an explanation of what the store had to offer, with special attention paid to jewelry. When the sales pitch ended I circled the store and made my way to the door for a quick exit, or so I thought. There must have been a watchman somewhere rubbing a brass lamp because that quickly a genie-like salesman appeared, certain that I would want to see their fine selection of carpets before I left. Do you see what I mean about the invisible sign somewhere over my head? However I was saved because two women traveling in the group heard the offer and expressed an interest in textiles! So Mr. Genie led them away and I was free to leave. It should be noted that my new friends bought three carpets!

Next stop, the beautiful island of Rhodes, home to the ancient Colossus, one of the seven wonders of the ancient world, and also home to a carpet store just outside the gate of the cruise ship yard. There are no accidents in the world of carpet merchandising! This store added a special touch. At its entrance there was a woman actually weaving a carpet before our eyes!

As we entered the store a lovely purple runner caught my eye! My Kusadasi carpet-buying friends and I spent some time in the store with a salesman named Socrates. In addition to the purple runner, there were several carpets that attracted my interest. Again I used the "a carpet is an investment" line, and again there was no pressure. We toured the medieval walled city and had lunch in a lovely taverna, while I considered buying the purple runner.

I returned to the store alone and looked at several other carpets, including a large area rug from Tabriz that was hanging on the wall. Socrates must have been out to lunch because a new salesman took care of me. Evidently Socrates must have told him to be on the lookout for me because he knew all about my interest in the purple carpet. Now that I had my eye on a larger (read: more expensive) carpet I was truly a person of interest and it only took a few moments for the salesman to remove the carpet from the wall and display it on the floor "as it should be seen." We talked about the price (and yes, if I included the purple runner a better price might be possible) and I had just about made up my mind to buy the carpet when I took one last walk-around. I am happy I did so, because I discovered some slight damage to the south-east corner of the carpet. I made the announcement that is every merchant's nightmare, "This carpet is damaged!" What followed was a flurry of activity that is hard to describe. It was as if I had announced the death of a family member. Socrates was called back from lunch and there was a frantic search for the carpet weaver who must have also taken a lunch break. I was assured by Socrates that the damage was not to the carpet itself but to the fringe area. It could be repaired and its value would not be compromised. I, however, was not moved and announced that I had lost all interest in the carpet. Even though I was sure that the carpet could be repaired and that its beauty and value would remain secure, they would certainly understand that I was not interested in purchasing a damaged carpet. A pall settled over the store and the purple runner was given center stage in a final effort to make a sale. I told Socrates that I had returned to the "I need to think about this" stage and left the store.

With that I was comfortable bringing my travels to a close and returning home without a carpet. After all, I did purchase several mementos all along the way that would serve as reminders of this most blessed trip. As you may have guessed, the story does not end with a damaged carpet in Rhodes!

While planning my travels, everyone I spoke with who had been to Greece said, "Be sure to visit the islands and do not miss Santorini!" I took their advice and arranged a tour that included Patmos and Ephesus, a must-see for me. I was fortunate to find a tour that also included Rhodes, Crete, Mykonos and a final stop in Santorini. They always save the best for last!

Santorini is the ancient Isle of Thira and is formed from the remains of a volcanic crater. We only had a few hours to visit so I opted not to take a tour of the island but to enjoy the village of Thira, located on the top of the mountain overlooking the sea. That meant that a tender boat took me to the coast and I had to take a cable car up the mountain! Shades of the open stairway experience at the Citadel of David filled my mind but I did not let that deter me. I have had previous experiences with cable cars and have learned that if I face the top of the hill the ride is not so traumatic. What I did not count on was the five visitors from France who shared the cable car with me. I claimed a safe seat facing up, but it seemed they were not able to experience the beautiful view in a seated position. One by one they stood up and "oohed and awed" at the natural beauty, all the while making the experience not unlike a visit to Hershey Park! I wanted to tell them that it was time to go home and vote for a new President but I did not want to interrupt the Sorrowful Mysteries I was praying. If anyone is interested, it takes three decades of the rosary to go from the coast to the top of the mountain. Of course, the presence of the jumping bean Frenchmen may have accelerated the rhythm of my prayer.

Santorini is everything people had promised, and more. The views of the harbor are breath-taking and the Orthodox Church of Candlemas has the most beautiful icons I have seen in all my travels. I took note of the names of several hotels (without balconies!) overlooking the harbor because I am sure I will return some day. I decided an early descent on the cable car might help me avoid another cabin of restless visitors, so after a few hours of walking through the town I made my way to the station. When I arrived at the cable car entrance my body turned left but my eyes turned right and caught sight of, you guessed it, a beautiful carpet inside a store named "Costas Dimitrokalis." How could you go wrong with a name that rhymes with Maria Callis?

The merchant welcomed me and told me that his name was Michael. That was not surprising since all men in Greece are named Nicholas, George, Demetrius or Michael. Michael told me that their carpets were made on the island. They are few in number since the younger generation does not seem interested in continuing the art. To make an already long story short, I found a rug to my liking, within in my price range, and made the purchase! Just as I was signing the credit card slip I heard someone in the doorway call out "Chet!" It was my Rhoades carpet-buying friends who just happened by as I sealed the deal! They approved of my purchase and later that evening, while sailing to Athens, we toasted to our carpet purchases.

Ancient Greek philosophers spoke of the search for the good, the true and the beautiful. It is a theme that later medieval theologians would develop when describing the virtuous life. There is something in the human spirit that both searches for, and creates beauty. Beauty comes in many forms. It might be a Renaissance painting, a rose in a bridal bouquet, or a child's scribble on the refrigerator door. One of my favorite poems reads: *If, of thy mortal goods, thou are bereft, And from thy slender store two loaves alone to thee are left, Sell one and from the dole, Buy Hyacinths to feed the soul. (Muslih-uddin Sadi)* I like to think that my carpet experiences are a part of the human search for beauty, and that in the years ahead my purchase will be hyacinths that feed my soul.

Thoughts On Leaving Greece – Attic Grace

Tomorrow I will leave Athens and travel to London for a week before setting sail for home; but today I am following my usual pattern and asking myself if there has been any one experience during my time here that stands out from all others. It is a difficult choice because the deeply spiritual visits to Patmos and Ephesus, the beauty of the Islands, and the friendliness of the Greek people have been especially memorable and meaningful. However, in naming one experience I would choose seeing the Attic funerary monuments in the National Archeological Museum.

The size and scope of the museum's collection is overwhelming; statuary, frescos, vases, pottery, and works in gold and bronze chronicle the history and mythology of Greece from its beginning in the Minoan world of King Minos on the island of Crete, to the Classical period and the Golden Age of Pericles in Athens. When I visit a museum for the first time I usually enter a room and spend time looking at just two or three items that immediately catch my eye, but in the rooms dedicated to the Funeral Stelai I could not choose. Each stele vied for my attention, and so I spent most of my time during both visits to the museums in those galleries.

The funerary monuments from the fourth and fifth century B.C. are highly stylized and follow a standard formula. Usually the dead person being memorialized is seated while being greeted with a handshake from a family member or household attendant. Two of the stelai are my favorites. The first shows an Athenian woman of noble birth examining a piece of her jewelry while here attendant stands nearby. The second is of an athlete mourning the death of his father. What I find to be most striking in each of these monuments is the serenity of both the deceased and those who mourn. There is sadness in the scenes but no one cries out and there is no exaggerated outpouring of grief. This is consistent with all the statuary of the Classical period. Individuals are shown in an idealized form, in the perfect balance that is the human ideal. That balance, that serenity, is what is referred to as "attic grace."

The great theologians of the Middle Ages built on the foundation of the ancient Greek philosophers. They borrowed the ideals of serenity and balance to develop a theology of the virtuous life, a life that follows the middle course, avoiding extremes on either side. That virtue, that balance, is visible in all Greek statuary of the Classical period but is most evident in the funerary monuments. I think that is why seeing the memorials made such a lasting impression on me. They represent the challenge we all face in trying to live a virtuous or balanced life. Sometimes we think about virtue as an extreme reality –goodness or kindness or honesty beyond the norm. But Virtue lies somewhere in the middle; it is never extreme. It represents a balanced approach to the challenges posed by a right way of living.

We do not have to search for that which is beyond our human reach to live a good life. We need only to avoid those extreme positions that cause us to lose our balance or force us to approach life with an exaggerated intensity that robs us of our psychic and spiritual energy. Many of those we admire as great saints are not those who did extraordinary things; rather they did ordinary things very well. Even those who did extraordinary things did so because they kept their balance in the doing.

I find that I often learn best when I can see the lesson being taught. The serenity of expression in the midst of great loss, displayed in the funerary monuments of the Classical Greek period tells me all that I need to know about living a balanced, virtuous life. It is a lesson that made my visits to the National Archeological Museum of Greece a most memorable experience.

And now it is off to London!

225

London

Seeing The Rosetta Stone –
Connecting The Dots

I remember studying it in World Cultures Class in the ninth grade. One inscription in three parallel languages – Greek, Hieroglyphics and Demotic. We call it the Rosetta Stone. Its discovery in 1799 provided scholars with a code for interpreting ancient Egyptian hieroglyphics. The Rosetta Stone is in the British Museum in London. I go to see this most important artifact each time I come to London. If I don't, I am afraid that my freshman history teacher, Sister Annunciata, will haunt me in my dreams!

With this recent visit to the British Museum I realized, that throughout my travels, I have often gone in search of an item of interest to the archeological world. In Rome, the "scavi" tour of the ancient cemetery underneath Saint Peter's Basilica provided an opportunity to see the inscription etched on a stone wall reading, "PETRUS ENI" – Peter is within. That simple phrase helped archeologists and historians to identify the tomb of the Apostle Peter.

I went to the Archeological Museum in Istanbul to see the "Siloam Stone," an inscription from the tunnel built by King Hezekiah in the 8th century B.C. that redirected Jerusalem's water supply during a pending attack by the Assyrians. The king's genius and industry helped to save the Holy City during a time of crisis.

In the Palace of Knosso on the island of Crete, I saw the "Fresco of the Bull" in the reconstructed labyrinth palace of King Minos. The scene provides insight into ancient religious practices in prehistoric Greece in the 18th century B.C.

In their study of the past, scholars often have very little to go on; perhaps a broken piece of pottery, remains of a mosaic, or fragments of an inscription on a stone pavement. By using their human ingenuity and the latest scientific technology, archeologists are able to piece together scant bits of information to provide a picture of ancient societies – how they dressed, what they ate, their way of warfare and methods for hunting and gathering.

What archeologists do in the practice of their science and art, I often do in reflecting on the meaning and purpose of my life. Trying to see the whole picture is difficult. It is like trying to watch ten movies at the same time. There are too many scenes, too many pictures at the same time and my mind can't process that much information. So most of the time I begin my reflection by remembering a particular event I have experienced or person I have met. Over time, after thinking about the specific happenings of my life *one at a time*, I am able draw conclusions or learn a life lesson. Just as an archeologist arranges his found objects like pieces of a puzzle and begins to see the bigger picture, I am able to see certain patterns emerge from the particulars of my life. It is like a puzzle book – when the dots are connected, a picture appears.

A song in the 60's asked, "What's it all about, Alfie? Is it just for the moment we live?" We do not live "just for the moment," but we do try to live "in each moment," because God is in the details of our lives. He meets us where we are living, not where we think we ought to be.

There are times when events from the past come into my consciousness, seemingly from nowhere and for no apparent reason. It might be a conversation I had with a friend from long ago, a movie that I saw last year, or a vacation I took to a far-away place. Upon reflection, the memory often brings new insights, or challenges me to think in a different way. I think God is at work in all of this. That is why memory played such an important part in the prayers of the Psalmist. When King David challenged the nation to remember, the chosen people saw the hand of God at work in the details of their history. So, too, with me. When I reflect on the particular people and events that have been a part of my life, I see a tapestry being woven by the hand of the master weaver; a tapestry that reveals a life that has meaning and purpose, even in the midst of uncertainty and disappointment.

Theologian David Tracy makes an interesting observation about literary works that are considered to be "classics" - works that have universal appeal in every age. Tracy says that these works have appeal not because their stories are so broad. In fact, the reverse is true. The classics are works that tell a story about a specific person wrestling with a particular problem at a given time in history. Spiritual writer Henri Nouwen says it this way, "What is most intimate is most universal."

That is why I think I have been sharing stories about particular events and individuals I have encountered throughout my sabbatical travels: the pizza clerk in Rome whose wife sends me kisses; the passing of the flame from the miracle of the fire on Holy Saturday in Jerusalem; walking down a metal staircase at the Citadel of David; shopping for a carpet in the Arasta Bazaar in Istanbul; my first view of the Acropolis on a sunny day in Athens. These individual stories are pieces of the puzzle and threads of the tapestry that has been my sabbatical journey. Sharing these events with you has helped me to connect the dots.

God Says Yes

Several years ago a study found that people visiting museums spend more time reading the labels on the paintings, sculptures and other artifacts, than they do looking at the objects themselves! I would make the same observation about people taking photographs. When they go home they are able to look at their picture albums, but I wonder if they can really say they actually saw the things they photographed.

The same might be said about aspects of my life of faith. Do I spend more time reading about prayer, than I do praying? Do I talk more *about* God, than I do talking *to* God? Do I take more care in planning the details of the liturgy than I do in preparing myself for our prayer together? In short, am I more religious, than I am spiritual? The words of Jesus come to mind, "The Sabbath was made for man, not man for the Sabbath." Are the externals of my faith in service to the interior life of the Spirit, or (in the spirit of the Pharisees) have I allowed my spiritual life to become enslaved by what can easily become the trappings of religion?

Jesus said that he came that we might have life, and have it to the full. (John 10:10) During his earthly ministry people were drawn to the person of Jesus. His words and actions encouraged and inspired them to enter into the relationship he had with his heavenly Father. Remember his powerful words at the Last Supper: *I no longer call you slaves, because a slave does not know what his master is doing. I have called you friends, because I have told you everything I have heard from my Father. (John 15:15)*

Often, I think, we have reduced our life of faith to a moral code, a way of behaving. The *relationship* that we have with Jesus is primary; it comes first. Our way of acting, our behavior, follows. We follow His law of love because we are His friends. We do not become friends of the Lord by following the law. Jesus' friendship is his gift to those he loves. I do not earn it, he gives it freely. That means that I ought to spend more time accepting, living and cherishing the friendship that Jesus has offered to me, than I do trying to prove myself worthy of it.

A friend of mine who loves and spoils here nieces once told me that she was going to spend a day with them and say "yes" to whatever they asked for! That is one of the privileges of being an aunt or uncle, a grandmother or grandfather! Of course, she was not going to agree to anything that would be harmful to them. She said that children hear "no" more often than they hear "yes." I wonder if her observation might be made about religion. Do I emphasize the "thou shall nots" of my faith rather than appreciate the fullness of life that is open to me because of God's generous love? When I do, I tend to cower in fear rather than live the "glorious freedom" that is mine as a child of God. I spend more time reading the labels, rather than looking at the art.

I believe that in the mystery of the Incarnation God changed humanity, God changed me, forever. When Jesus became one like us, when he died and rose again to new life, the doors of Paradise were reopened forever. I am no longer on the outside looking in. "I am God's child NOW," Saint Paul reassures me. The glorious reign of the kingdom of God will be brought to fulfillment when Christ returns at then end of time as we know it. Until then, I need to remember that the kingdom has already begun and, through my baptism into Christ Jesus, I share in it NOW. As a result I am free to take a long, loving look at the face of Christ. I can stop reading the labels.

On Leaving London – A Final Thought

One morning in Jerusalem a button was coming off the shirt that I wanted to wear that day. In comparison to all that is happening in the Middle East, this was certainly not a big problem. Besides, perhaps because she foresaw my future celibate state, in her wisdom my mother had taught me how to cook, to do laundry, and to sew buttons on a shirt. It should be noted that my mother was not a fan of sewing. "The pin people have to live too," was one of her favorite sayings.

My years as a Boy Scout had taught me to "be prepared," and so I had packed a small travel sewing kit. The crisis came when I had to thread the needle. On and off came my multi-field eyeglasses as I tried to accomplish what should have been a five minute chore. I even had the benefit of a small "threader" (not sure what the technical term is) but you still have to get that small wire loop through the even smaller eye of the needle. It took about thirty minutes and my words that were matter for confession, but I finally succeeded and was able to reattach the button.

On this, my last day in London before sailing home, I discovered that another button on another shirt was hanging by a thread. So I prepared myself for another session of needle-threading frustration. The hotel had supplied a small sewing kit next to the shower cap (does anybody ever wear those things?) and I decided to make good use of the grant money and use the one provided. Am I glad I did! God bless Mr. Marriott! For in the kit he provided, the needles were already threaded; six needles with six colors of just enough thread to meet any emergency sewing need. What a brilliant idea! Whoever thought of this one deserves a Nobel Prize, or at least a plenary indulgence for keeping me from another occasion of sin!

Tomorrow I will be clicking the heels of the ruby slippers and saying, "there is no place like home" as I set sail for the American shores. Before I do, I have this feeling that I should be offering some profound final reflection summarizing these past months of study and travel. As I have shared before, I believe that lessons from this sabbatical journey will continue to be learned long after I have returned home. Memories will surface and new insights will be gained in the weeks, months and years ahead. However I will share one concluding thought.

Having a friendship with God, through our baptism into his Son Jesus, means that as part of the human condition (read: this 'ain't heaven yet) we are going to encounter obstacles and frustration in the challenges that life presents to us. But it also means that most of the time we are going to find that the needle has already been threaded and we have been provided with enough grace to meet the challenge at hand. Jesus has promised that he would not leave us orphans; he would send his Spirit who would teach us all that we need to know. It is a promise we celebrate with great solemnity on the feast of Pentecost. So, when we seem to be hanging on by a thread, like the buttons on my shirt in Jerusalem and London, we have to remember that we are not limited by the eyeglasses of our limited human vision. Rather, we have the insight of the Holy Spirit to lead and guide us through whatever challenge, large or small, we are facing at the moment. As people of faith, we will discover that most of the time the needle has already been threaded.

Now it is off to America. And in case you are concerned, I am not wearing ruby slippers!

Printed in the United States
133464LV00004B/301-393/P

9 781438 933368